C000257949

Export Growth in Latin America

Published in cooperation with the
Economic Commission for Latin America and the Caribbean

Export Growth in Latin America

Policies and Performance

Carla Macario
with Regis Bonelli, Adriaan ten Kate, and Gunnar Niels

BOULDER
LONDON

Published in the United States of America in 2000 by
Lynne Rienner Publishers, Inc.
1800 30th Street, Boulder, Colorado 80301
www.rienner.com

and in the United Kingdom by
Lynne Rienner Publishers, Inc.
3 Henrietta Street, Covent Garden, London WC2E 8LU

The responsibility for opinions expressed in these studies rests solely with their authors, and their publication does not constitute an endorsement by the United Nations.

Library of Congress Cataloging-in-Publication Data
Export growth in Latin America : policies and performance / Carla Macario with Regis Bonelli, Adriaan ten Kate, and Gunnar Niels.
Includes bibliographical references and index.
ISBN 1-55587-759-1 (hc. : alk. paper)
1. Exports—Latin America—Case studies. 2. Latin America—Commercial policy.
HF3230.5.Z5 M33 2000
382'.6'098—dc21 00-028260

British Cataloguing in Publication Data
A Cataloguing in Publication record for this book is available from the British Library.

Printed and bound in the United States of America

The paper used in this publication meets the requirements of the American National Standard for Permanence of Paper for Printed Library Materials Z39.48-1984.

5 4 3 2 1

Contents

Acknowledgments

This book originated in the Regional Project on Policies to Promote Innovation and Competitiveness in the Latin American and Caribbean Business Sector (RLA/88/039), carried out by the Economic Commission for Latin America and the Caribbean (ECLAC) and financed by the United Nations Development Programme.

I would like to thank Wilson Peres, chief of the Industrial and Technological Development Unit and head of the project, and Jorge Katz, director of the Division of Production, Productivity and Management at ECLAC, for the support they provided throughout the entire process. Hector Assael was very helpful and made insightful comments. I would also like to express my gratitude to Joseph Ramos for having initially identified some of the main issues addressed in the study and, above all, for his constant encouragement.

—*C. M.*

1

Introduction

Carla Macario

Latin American and Caribbean countries have substantially transformed their economies over the past decades by adopting policies that foster a greater outward orientation of their economies and by setting aside import substitution development strategies. While the intensity of the transformations varies across countries, the region has definitely shifted development models. Macroeconomic and trade policy reforms are at the center of the changes that have taken place.

One of the foundations of the development strategy adopted by Latin American countries is the high priority assigned to increasing exports. Exports have certainly increased from US$104 billion in 1987 to US$279 billion in 1997. Nevertheless, that expansion is partly due to the growth of exports from one country, Mexico. In fact, the region's share in world merchandise trade declined from 5.8% in 1983 to 5.3% in 1997: Latin America's share, excluding Mexico, was only 3.2% for that last year, which is practically the same as in 1990 (3.1%), according to the World Trade Organization (WTO 1998a). Therefore, Latin American countries are not taking full advantage of the opportunities that result from the increase of global trade.

Moreover, according to the Economic Commission for Latin America and the Caribbean, primary commodities still make up an important share of the countries' exports for most countries, excluding Barbados, Brazil, and Mexico (ECLAC 1999a). In consequence, Latin American and Caribbean economies are highly vulnerable to the fluctuations of the global economy. This export specialization is also undesirable in the long run because the prices of commodities relative to those of manufactured goods will continue to decline during the coming decades (World Bank 1999).

The counterpart to Latin America's enduring specialization in exporting primary commodities is the region's inability to have manufactured exports grow at high rates. For the vast majority of Latin American countries, exports of goods with higher levels of value added tend to decrease as the domestic demand recovers and the exchange rate appreciates. The region's poor performance regarding manufactured exports is one of the explanations for its inability to benefit from the expansion of global trade, since trade of manufactured exports grows at a much higher rate than other exports. For instance, manufactured exports grew at 7% per year from 1990 to 1997, while agricultural and mining exports grew at a rate of 4.5% for the same period (WTO 1998b).

Mexico—which has had a spectacular export performance during recent years—is the most notable exception to the specialization in exporting commodities. The share of Mexico's exports in merchandise exports from Latin America has risen during the past several years to 43% in 1998. The main explanations for Mexico's outstanding export performance are the close links to the U.S. market that were strengthened by the North American Free Trade Agreement (NAFTA) and specialization in exporting manufactured goods.

The differences in export specialization have significant consequences for trade performance: Latin America's merchandise exports, excluding those of Mexico, dropped by 7% in 1998, but Mexico's have increased by 6.5%. That country's exports have systematically grown at higher rates than exports from the rest of the region over the past few years (WTO 1999).

Additionally, Latin America's being weak in manufactured exports has momentous consequences by insulating it from the dynamic growth-stimulating effects of manufacturing for export, such as the "learning effects, the realization of scale economies and the creation of positive externalities associated with manufacturing for export" (Helleiner 1995).

Therefore, the question at issue is which policies have the potential of encouraging a higher export growth rate, particularly for manufactured exports. Achieving this goal would allow Latin American and Caribbean countries to take greater advantage of the opportunities arising from the increase of global trade. At the same time, these countries could benefit from the positive spillover effects of manufacturing for export.

Latin American governments have started to assign a greater priority to export growth policies during recent years. There is a growing recognition that while macroeconomic and trade policy reforms are essential for improving export growth, they are not sufficient for encouraging a sustainable increase of manufactured exports.

The export promotion policies that have customarily been used by the countries in the region have, for the most part, become insufficient for addressing the challenges faced by export firms nowadays. More needs to be done if the region wishes to reap the benefits of the surge of global trade.

Together with that, the updated export promotion policies need to be compatible with the Uruguay Round Agreements. These agreements have benefited developing countries by increasing trade opportunities and strengthening the dispute settlement procedures, and have established new rules for nonagricultural export subsidies, which will be progressively cut. The new rules—to be enforced by the WTO—will lead to important changes in policy, many of them beneficial to developing countries in the present circumstances.

One of the consequences of the WTO rules is that the new export promotion policies will have to emphasize addressing the source of the inefficiencies that originally justified setting up export subsidies. The new rules governing multilateral trade allow governments to resist the pressures of lobbies and to move toward policies that address inefficiencies at the source and seek to increase firms' ability to export on a sustainable basis. Similarly, many of the policies traditionally used to set up export-processing zones will have to be modified. Therefore, export promotion policies will become more relevant than in the past, as other instruments are eliminated.

Hence, most countries in the region will have to revise their export promotion policies to ensure that the policies will be fully compatible with the new multilateral trade rules by the year 2003. The new set of export promotion policies needs to be effective—in tune with the new policy environment and consistent with the new multilateral trade rules.

This book seeks to contribute to the discussions of policymakers regarding which policies would be most appropriate for encouraging export growth in Latin America. The approach used here is to combine an examination of a country's export promotion policies with microeconomic research. The case studies were carried out in firms that export manufactured goods with relatively high levels of value added, at least when compared to the region's exports. The purpose was to learn from the companies that are successful exporters and to assess the effectiveness of export promotion policies from the viewpoint of the final users, that is export firms themselves. This procedure is rarely used to evaluate the effectiveness of policy instruments.

At the same time, carrying out company-based studies has the additional benefit of improving the knowledge of firms' behavior in the context of the present macroeconomic and trade policies. The abundance of macroeconomic studies over the past years stands in contrast to the scarcity of the research on how Latin American firms have changed their behavior in response to the macroeconomic and trade policy changes.

One of the first microeconomic studies examined how Chilean firms had adapted to the macroeconomic and trade policy changes during the 1970s and early 1980s (Corbo and Sánchez 1984). In recent years, there has been a growing interest in conducting research into the changes in manufacturing companies' behavior and the way they are adapting to the new economic environment.[1] Nevertheless, the evidence about the microeconomic changes in Latin America following the changes in macroeconomic and trade policy is still lacking. This volume seeks to provide information that helps to fill that gap, and should be useful for academics and analysts interested in the behavior of Latin American manufacturing companies.

All the same, it is important to point out that the approach used for the country studies has the disadvantage of working with a sample that is not statistically representative, thus producing weaker conclusions than those based on econometric analysis. Moreover, there is an evident selection bias, because most of the studies focused on companies that were successful at exporting.

Despite these limitations, the procedure used here has the advantage of providing an abundance of information at the microeconomic level that is very useful for designing export promotion instruments. These instruments are designed to be used by individual companies. If the knowledge of how export companies behave is inadequate, the policy instruments may be off target and therefore ineffective.

This book presents country studies of Brazil, Chile, Colombia, and Mexico. It was essential to include Brazil and Mexico because they are the two leading exporters in Latin America. Mexico is also the only country in the region that exports significant amounts of manufactured goods, in spite of having been essentially a primary goods exporter as recently as the early 1980s. For an investigation of policies that successfully encourage manufactured exports, Mexico is clearly the first choice among Latin American and Caribbean countries.[2]

Chile was one of the first countries in the region to adopt an outward-oriented strategy. It was also a forerunner in export promotion policies. Both Chile and Mexico have export promotion policies that are effective and, for the most part, compatible with the new rules that will be enforced by the WTO. Colombia is included in the country studies because it was one of the first nations in Latin America to have effective export promotion policies. Study of these four countries allows a good geographical sample of the medium and large economies of the region.

The remainder of Chapter 1 highlights certain points of the debate about economies of scale and learning by exporting, from the perspective of thinking about policies for export growth. It briefly reviews some of the findings of the country studies regarding the main questions addressed by the project, and is but a concise summary aimed at prompting a first discussion of these issues. It is not intended as an exhaustive presentation; each chapter discusses additional topics directly relevant to the specific country.

Chapters 2 to 5 examine the policies that are determinants for export performance in the four named Latin American countries. The chapters describe the macroeconomic environment and trade policy and detail export promotion instruments in these countries. They also discuss the influence of these policies on the behavior of export firms so as to derive conclusions relevant for formulating policy recommendations aimed at enhancing export performance. Chapter 6 sets forth policy recommendations aimed at increasing exports based on the results of the country studies.

Economies of Scale and Learning by Exporting: A Review of the Literature

For many years, the fundamental principles of trade theory were the models presented by David Ricardo and by Eli Heckscher and Bertil Ohlin. Ricardo's model demonstrated that trade among countries was driven by the differences between relative prices. Heckscher and Ohlin's model established that countries would specialize in exporting goods relatively intensive in the production factors they were most abundant in prior to trade and that—in the long run—trade tends to equalize factor returns (Caves and Jones 1985). Along with these two models, there are many others in traditional trade theory that have made key contributions to the understanding of the main features of trade flows in the world, particularly interindustry trade.

Nevertheless, traditional trade theory cannot provide an explanation for the discrepancy between the Heckscher-Ohlin-based models' prediction about factor return equalization and what can be observed in the real world. It cannot predict the growing importance of intraindustry trade between industrialized nations or of intrafirm trade by multinational corporations. Furthermore, there is a confusion between positive and normative issues when the Heckscher and Ohlin model's prediction that countries with abundant labor will specialize in exporting labor-intensive goods gets turned into a policy recommendation suggesting that developing countries should specialize in exporting this kind of merchandise (Bhagwati and Srinivasan 1983).

The inconsistency between traditional trade theory's predictions and the stylized facts characterizing trade flows today became more acute in light of the remarkable growth of manufactured exports from the newly industrializing countries in Southeast Asia. Far from specializing permanently in exporting goods for which they had an initial comparative advantage, these countries decided to build the capability to progressively modify their comparative advantage. Traditional trade theory—based on the assumptions of perfect competition, perfect information, homogeneous products, and constant returns to scale—was not very useful when analyzing the changes that were taking place and was even less so when it came to thinking about the policy implications.

In response to these lacunae, efforts were made during the 1970s and the 1980s to develop international trade models that no longer systematically included the restrictive assumptions mentioned above. The models introduced concepts from the theory of industrial organization, thus allowing for imperfect competition, increasing returns to scale, product differentiation, and asymmetric information (Ethier 1979; Brander and Spencer 1985; Horstmann and Markusen 1992; Brainard 1993; Neary 1994). The models' purpose is to show that trade is not always driven by comparative advantage but can also result from increasing returns to scale within the firm, from external economies, and/or from imperfect competition. The models' significant contribution to economic theory is that trade models presently have a greater consistency with some of the stylized facts currently observed, such as intraindustry trade.

Paul Krugman's pioneer work played a particularly important role in this improvement by developing techniques that allowed a formal introduction of economies of scale in trade models. He demonstrated, for example, that an early start in producing a good can allow a country to acquire an advantage in that industry through dynamic increasing returns—external economies that are obtained throughout time—as the industry accumulates knowledge (Krugman 1987; Krugman and Obstfeld 1994). When the industry spends more time producing the good, it can decrease average cost due to past experience (learning by doing) and specialize in the production of that good. History may matter more than initial comparative advantage.

Hence, it may be that specialization results not only from an initial static comparative advantage but also from economies of scale within the firm or the industry, from an early start in producing a good, or from a temporary shock that promotes (or destroys) a given industry. Thus temporary shocks can have permanent effects on trade.

Alwyn Young (1991) discusses the dynamic effects of international trade with an endogenous growth model in which learning by doing, while being bounded for each good, has positive spillovers across goods. This model is useful for analyzing the learning that takes place over time as firms learn how to export, which allows them to acquire permanent comparative advantages as long as the learning cannot be totally captured across borders or internationalized. The greater the link between the dynamic economies of scale and country-specific characteristics that cannot be easily transferred, such as human capital or an efficient institutional support system, the greater the comparative advantage that the industry can acquire. Inversely, if the knowledge can easily be copied, such as what variety of asparagus is the best for exports or which are the countries that are the best purchasers, the country will have difficulty in maintaining its comparative advantage. Other nations will benefit from its pioneer export activities.

Many of the new trade theory models presented by economists in industrialized countries appear to be a mere formalized version of issues that have been discussed for years by economists interested in development economics, such as industrialization by import substitution and infant industries. Dani Rodrik (1988) points out that "this new literature is a frustrating reminder to the south that too often ideas become intellectually respectable only when they become congruent with the interest of major northern countries."

Yet, the new models do present the outstanding advantage of attempting to set up in a formal way issues that had up to now not been presented in such a form. They also contribute to bringing back to the center of the discussion of economic analysis topics that, while being relevant for developing countries, had been excluded from the mainstream of the economic theory due to the lack of rigorous economic models.

From a different perspective, Jorge Katz (1987) carried out research on the economics of technology generation in the largest Latin American countries. His investigation in individual firms yields an evolutionary path for "in-house" technological search efforts, as companies try to adapt technologies designed for firms in industrialized nations. Once this learning path is followed, the companies have a technology that is functional for domestic conditions. Therefore, they are then able to export the adapted technologies to neighboring countries, given that these technologies will also tend to be more appropriate for firms in those nations. From that perspective, "technological learning in the domestic industrial sector could give rise to a sequence of exports of increasing technical sophistication" (Ablin and Katz 1987). Although these studies are not carried out in the framework of the new trade theory, but rather in that of evolutionary economics, they also depart from standard neoclassical theory by proceeding to lift assumptions.

At the outset, the new trade theory was thought out from a positive perspective, which is to provide models with predictions that are more consistent with the observed stylized facts. The goal was not a normative one. However, the policy implications of these new models have been at the center of intense discussions. This is particularly the case of the strategic trade policy.

The general idea behind the strategic trade policy is that a home country that is initially less competitive than a foreign country in a given industry could shift its comparative advantage by temporarily closing down its economy. This would enable it to protect the domestic industry, thus allowing it to become more productive until it reaches the productivity level of the foreign country. Krugman has pointed out that he believes that the strategic trade policy argument should not be considered a major contribution of the new trade theory since it cannot be proven that deviating from free trade provides countries with substantial gains (Krugman 1993; Helpman 1989).

What are the implications of the new trade theory models for developing countries today? Without discussing whether strategic trade policy is beneficial to large industrialized nations, it clearly is not appropriate for the Latin American economies given that they have relatively small domestic markets. The limited size of the domestic market would hinder firms from attaining a level of output where they could have substantial economies of scale if they were temporarily protected from import competition. That is precisely one of the stumbling blocks to the import substitution development strategy.

In addition, the welfare loss to consumers because of protection, even temporary, would be significant. Moreover, an increase of protection would be incompatible with the macroeconomic and trade policy reforms in Latin American countries during the past decades. Finally, the difficulty of designing appropriate policies within the framework of strategic trade policy and of avoiding its benefits from being captured by special-interest groups is certainly not negligible. Therefore, the costs of protection would be clearly higher than the benefits.

However, the fact that strategic trade policy is not relevant for developing countries does not imply that the same conclusion can be reached for economies of scale. While increasing returns to scale have mainly been used to explain intraindustry trade between industrialized nations, the fact that intraindustry trade is not as significant for developing countries does not imply that economies of scale are irrelevant for developing nations. In these countries increasing returns explain some flows of interindustry trade: for smaller economies, an efficient plant size may produce a level of output that is bigger than the size of the domestic market. Since the degree of specialization is not as high as in industrialized countries, interindustry trade may be relatively more important than intraindustry trade. On the other hand, as preferential trade agreements expand the size of regional markets, intraindustry trade may become more important between the members of the agreements.

Economies of scale have figured prominently in the discussion regarding the improvement of resource allocation in developing countries. Anne Krueger (1985) indicates that the possibility of exploiting economies of scale is one of the reasons why export-oriented development strategies have enabled Asian exporters to achieve higher growth rates than countries following import substitution strategies.

José Antonio Ocampo (1993) points out that the new trade theory has implications for trade policy in developing countries: liberalizing trade between developing nations allows them to take advantage of the different economies of scale discussed by these models. Regional preferential trade agreements also allow firms to have access to larger markets and therefore to benefit from economies of scale (Devlin and Ffrench-Davis 1999).

It must be pointed out that the initial impact of trade liberalization on economies of scale is not straightforward. Although it is true that domestic firms in industries with increasing returns may potentially achieve economies of scale when countries open up their economies, the impact may be ambiguous. Trade liberalization may destroy industries that had previously had access to economies of scale as long as the domestic market was protected (Rodrik 1992).

Yet, when the discussion turns away from the topic of whether trade liberalization will always result in resource allocation gains—or if these gains are also the product of the sound macroeconomic policies that accompanied trade liberalization—to that of analyzing the case of firms that not only survived the opening up of the economy but effectively are exporting, and of comparing them to firms that do not sell abroad once trade has been liberalized for several years already, the ambiguity decreases. One could expect export firms to have a decrease in their unit cost as their output increases due to increased exports, if the technology used in the industry allows for increasing returns.

Therefore, the perspective provided by the new trade theory models is particularly useful for developing countries when analyzing those economies of scale that arise while exporting. These can be the most frequently mentioned economies of scale—static economies of scale ensuing, for example, from a greater production capability due to larger plants—together with dynamic economies of scale resulting from investment over time and from knowledge accumulation through learning by doing.

Hence, while one policy conclusion that could be derived from the new trade theory models in industrialized nations is to suggest that in some industries it is advisable to temporarily protect domestic firms to ensure them economies of scale that allow an increase in productivity, these same models lead to radically different policy recommendations for developing countries with smaller domestic markets.

In fact, the policy recommendation in developing countries for industries that have the potential to benefit from economies of scale is exactly the opposite. The firms that should receive temporary assistance should not be those producing mainly for the domestic market. On the contrary, support should be available for export firms that have access to a larger market when exporting: selling abroad allows such companies to attain greater economies of scale. It also enables firms to get on a steeper learning curve because they are exposed to highly demanding clients, the most advanced technologies, and updated product specifications and marketing strategies. Inasmuch as there are potential benefits that can be obtained by putting firms on steeper learning curves and having access to a larger market, it is export firms that should receive assistance.

Moreover, upgrading technology in manufacturing often implies larger scales of plants and of companies (Alcorta 1994). Furthermore, economies of scale can also play a role as a firm increases its international marketing capability (Keesing and Lall 1992). There are specific economies of scale directly related to exporting, for example, resulting from a fixed cost such as having an export division. At the same time, there are external economies as more companies get information on how to export and on new markets.

The externalities resulting from pioneer export firms' activities are an additional justification for providing assistance for these companies. Marketing abroad is an expensive and demanding activity for pioneer firms that benefits latecomers as they enter markets where the first successful firms have already shown the way and borne most of the initial costs and risks. This is particularly true for information costs. The fact that pioneer firms cannot capture all the benefits of their initial incursion into world markets results in a level of exports that is suboptimal.

The role of knowledge accumulation and learning by doing in growth and trade models has become more relevant in the recent years (Lucas 1993; Krugman 1987; Krugman and Obstfeld 1994).[3] At the same time, certain econometric studies have concluded that there is no evidence that firms learn from exporting (Clerides, Lach, and Tybout 1998; Roberts and Tybout 1997 discussed by Westphal [1998]).

Larry Westphal questions the results from these aggregate data investigations by pointing out that they contradict the evidence from an abundance of findings from case studies. He believes that the link between high exports and remarkable development performance results from the "unrivaled benefits in the form of accelerated and efficacious technological development that can be derived through aggressive export activity" (Westphal 2225).

An empirical confirmation of the importance that purposefully oriented learning has for developing countries is provided by the experience of the East Asian countries: "What the whole East Asian experience has been about is learning, entering global markets at the low end, moving up and taking advantages of the learning which comes with playing in the global market" (Barry 1989).

Concurrently, Michael Hobday (1995) provides a thorough description of the exceptional learning process undertaken by electronic firms in East Asia. Exporting pushed these companies to upgrade their technological and marketing skills to be able to satisfy requirements more demanding than those in the domestic markets.

The additional exposure to learning opportunities when selling abroad appears to be particularly significant for exports of products with relatively high value added. Exporting these products often demands a greater technological knowledge that can in turn have positive spillovers for the rest of the economy. This is now an important issue for Latin American countries.

In sum, economies of scale and learning by doing are at the center of some of the issues discussed by mainstream economic theory. The investigation in Brazil, Chile, Colombia, and Mexico was designed to establish whether these topics are relevant for successful Latin American export companies. It also examined other subjects that are critical for firms' export performance and for effective export promotion policies.

Issues Covered in This Book

The rest of this chapter summarizes some of the points addressed by the country studies. It does not intend, however, to cover all the topics discussed in the following chapters. The questions asked here are the following: Do firms that export regularly have access to greater economies of scale than companies focused mainly on the domestic market? Do export companies have—over time—greater learning opportunities than nonexport firms, thus exhibiting dynamic economies of scale through knowledge accumulation? What export promotion policies are most effective for assisting export firms? What are the chief obstacles faced by exporters? This section also discusses the importance of the exchange rate for export performance.

Economies of Scale

The link between economies of scale and exporting is strong in Chile and Colombia. Selling abroad allows export firms in these countries to have access to greater economies of scale than the companies that focus mainly on the domestic market. Hence there is a connection between exporting and economies of scale, at least in these smaller economies.

The causality link goes in both directions. Export firms have access to greater economies of scale than the companies that sell mainly in the domestic market precisely because they export. Concurrently, economies of scale at the plant level push firms to export.

Along the same line, the introduction of updated technologies often implies a larger scale. Manufacturing companies need to improve the quality of the goods they manufacture. If they fail to do so, they face the prospect of losing market share to imported goods and of eventually having to close their plants. However, manufacturing higher quality goods requires the use of updated technologies. This in turn often implies a substantial increase in the scale of the plant. Hence, for the Latin American countries with relatively small domestic markets, manufacturing will increasingly require exporting.

By contrast, the connection between selling abroad and economies of scale was weak in Brazil and Mexico, where economies of scale were not a significant factor for export decisions for the industries included in the project. The larger size of these two economies implies that for many industries, the domestic market is large enough to permit economies of scale. This conclusion is obviously strongly dependent on the industry: car manufacturing, for example, requires a market size much larger than the domestic one in both these nations.

Rather than economies of scale, the determining factor that triggered exports by the Mexican firms covered by the study was the decrease of demand in the domestic market. Economic recessions are the single most important factor that initially pushed Mexican firms to start exporting, irrespective of what industry they engage in. Most of the companies covered by the project (which excluded transnational corporations) had not initially needed to invest large sums in expanding manufacturing capacity to begin to export. In fact, the companies started exporting to use excess capacity after domestic demand plummeted in the country's successive recessions.[4] This is clearly a case of "switching" of sales from the domestic market to external markets in response to depressed domestic demand (Helleiner 1995).

In any event, for the smaller economies in Latin America the connection between exporting and economies of scale matters. Manufacturing firms in these countries will increasingly have to consider exporting if they want to remain in the manufacturing business as their countries progressively open their markets to trade and investment.

Learning by Exporting

Exporting—by exposing firms to international competition and to greater information—provides companies with considerable learning opportunities. This learning takes place in export-related activities, as could have been expected, and in other areas that are not directly connected to exporting. Therefore, export firms can get on a steeper learning curve than firms that sell mainly in the domestic market. Exporting encourages companies to upgrade and at the same time provides them with greater information about the changes needed to accomplish that goal. The evidence presented in the country studies strongly corroborates Westphal's conviction and Hobday's findings concerning the importance of exporting for providing firms with learning opportunities. This was particularly clear in Chile, demonstrated by a comparison of export firms with companies that focused mainly on the domestic market.

Selling abroad enables companies' access to information on the main trends in global markets, updated product specifications and quality control procedures, input procurement sources, and leading production, management, and marketing practices. Thus these companies have more information than nonexport firms.

In addition to enhanced information opportunities, exporting requires firms to change their practices and learn to do things differently. This is particularly true for firms that sell to large companies with supplier certification programs, which provide assistance for upgrading production and management practices. Exporting has a strong impact on firms, pushing them to upgrade and providing them with better information on the steps to take in that direction.

The single most significant point is that clients in export markets are generally much more demanding than those in the domestic market. Quality control is a critical issue: exporting forces companies to significantly upgrade the quality of their merchandise and to put in place stringent quality control systems.

In sum, the learning process that takes place in exporting firms allows them to have access to dynamic economies of scale that enables them to gain market share in export markets as well as the domestic market. Moreover, the learning process stimulated by exporting has positive spillovers in the domestic market, allowing the companies to introduce updated products and practices.

Nevertheless, although export companies in Colombia had greater learning opportunities than firms selling exclusively in the domestic market, entrepreneurs could not take full advantage of these opportunities. This was because Colombian executives had to spend a considerable amount of time and energy overcoming the obstacles faced by their companies. Another factor that curtailed the learning opportunities provided by exporting was the difficulty firms had when importing inputs. Finally, the fact that import competition in Colombia is at this time moderate also contributes to the lower degree of learning.

This last point can be linked to another conclusion, one that was not initially expected, but which ex post makes sense. Even if exporting provides firms with greater learning opportunities than selling only on the domestic market, it is also true that there are other enhanced learning opportunities. These are opportunities that result from selling in a domestic market with an intense degree of competition or from being suppliers to industries that are striving in export markets.

For instance, the study in Chile showed that as the economy has progressively become more open to competition because of trade liberalization, the appreciation of the exchange rate, the strong increase in per capita income, and an influx of new distribution networks, there has been a blurring of the difference between the behavior of export firms and that of the companies that sell mainly on the domestic market. The growing degree of competition in the domestic market is pushing a greater proportion of manufacturing firm managers to operate more like export company managers. These managers are looking for the best input sources and hiring consultants with the goal of changing product specifications and production and management practices. Moreover, firm executives are now frequently going to trade fairs and traveling abroad to visit other companies in the same industry. For instance, the intense degree of competition in the printing market in Chile has allowed companies that managed to be successful in the domestic market to then export without having to substantially change the specifications of their products. Therefore, a greater degree of competition in the domestic market is effectively a good way of encouraging firms to have a more active approach toward upgrading.

At the same time, the research in Brazil and in Mexico showed that while direct exporters had greater learning opportunities than firms catering mainly to the domestic market, there were also significant learning opportunities arising from supplying world-class exporting companies. For example, the firms that have managed to successfully supply companies manufacturing automobiles in the two countries were then capable of exporting without having to substantially modify their products. The upgrading opportunities were directly proportional to the strength of the links between the firms manufacturing auto parts and the large automobile assembly companies. In that sense, the point that manufacturing for export is the best way to encourage learning and enable upgrading remains valid. However, the exporting need not be direct but may be indirect too.

Nevertheless, these enhanced learning opportunities are for the most part confined to a few industries in the region, mainly in Brazil and Mexico. Most other countries have yet to develop industries that manufacture products capable of meeting international standards. On the other hand, this strongly confirms the idea that attracting investment in high-technology industries can have positive externalities.

Hence, learning is stimulated by competition and the exposure to demanding product standards. This learning can result from intense domestic competition or from the possibility of supplying world-class exporters. Increasing competition in the domestic market and attracting companies that are among the top players in manufactured goods export markets is a good way of encouraging firms to learn and upgrade.

Exporting provides companies with the foremost learning and upgrading opportunities. Therefore, encouraging firms to export and supplying them with assistance to do so is a way of inducing companies to upgrade and facilitating the process.

Export Promotion Policies[5]

Export promotion assistance is most effective for companies that are beginning to export when information is readily available and export formalities are transparent, streamlined, and expeditious, as in Chile and Mexico. Trade promotion organizations' assistance for going to trade fairs and marketing abroad is highly beneficial for small and medium companies.

Adequate export financing, such as provided by BANCOLDEX in Colombia and BANCOMEXT in Mexico, is critical for firms' export capability. Moreover, export credit availability acquires greater significance as export subsidies are phased out to comply with the Uruguay Round Agreements. Therefore, the decision of the government of Brazil to emphasize the development of export financing will allow more firms in that country to break into export markets, as long as the financial assistance procedures are clearly established and access is facilitated for a wide range of companies.

At the same time, systematic and recurrent efforts to further decrease the antiexport bias encourage a greater number of firms to export. Therefore, Latin American countries should continue their progress in that direction. They should also have a policy environment that encourages widespread productivity increases in the economy, thus allowing an upgrade of the country's export supply capability.

Last, the importance of having a strategy for increasing export growth that has a high priority in a government's agenda and that is coherent with the other key policies in the country cannot be overemphasized. Export promotion policies by themselves are not sufficient for triggering export growth. An increase of the rate of growth of manufactured exports that persists over time—even when domestic demand recovers and when the exchange rate appreciates—requires a comprehensive strategy.

Export Obstacles

Several Latin American countries have made significant progress in reducing the disincentives to exporting by decreasing the obstacles that entrepreneurs face when they sell abroad. Yet, the numerous difficulties met by exporters remain an important stumbling block that curtails export growth in the majority of the countries of the region.

To address this issue Brazil and Costa Rica, for example, have given a high priority to measures aimed at cutting the *costo país,* that is, the additional cost firms bear when exporting from that country. Mexico, with its impressive reduction of export red tape, has a commission—the Comisión Mixta para la Promoción de Exportaciones (COMPEX)—set up to reduce the bottlenecks faced by exporters.

Brazilian firms face a maze of regulations administered by different agencies. Furthermore, the excessive bureaucracy encountered by export firms has increased during the past years due to the intricacy of the requirements for issuing certificates of origin for Mercosur. In Colombia, the complexity of the red tape required to get goods through customs has curtailed the impact of trade liberalization. Mexican and Chilean firms do not have to go through much paperwork when selling abroad, but they face substantial red tape when exporting to other countries in Latin America because of the regulations in the importing nations. Exporting to the United States, in contrast, is often less cumbersome.

Excessive paperwork is an obstacle to exporting that can be substantially reduced at very little cost. It does require, however, that governments have the political will to eliminate the paperwork and overcome the resistance from agencies trying to preserve their discretionary powers.

Infrastructure deficiencies strongly contribute to increasing the costs faced by export firms. The high costs of and the delays to getting goods through the port of Santos in Brazil have long had the reputation of being the best barrier against import competition. Chilean firms exporting manufactured goods to neighboring countries sometimes have to delay shipments due to roads that are not open all year long. There are many similar examples in most Latin American countries. Such inefficiencies are a significant obstacle to increasing export growth.

Governments wanting to increase export growth should consider investing in improving the infrastructure needed by export firms. These investments could be financed by a reallocation of the funds that will be available as export subsidies are phased out. After all, this is precisely the kind of obstacle to exports that justified setting up the subsidies in the first place. Eliminating the source of the inefficiency would be the best use for these funds, and doing so will contribute to a widespread cost reduction in the economy.

The Influence of the Exchange Rate

The evolution of the exchange rate is critical for export performance. It affects companies' ability to get export orders for the goods that they are manufacturing at present. Moreover, it has long-term consequences because of its influence on the decisions of whether or not to invest in export-oriented industries. An exchange rate policy that provides incentives leading to exporting and investing in export industries is essential for increasing manufactured exports (Helleiner 1995). All the same, several countries in Latin America have allowed the exchange rate to appreciate in order to achieve goals other than promoting export growth. Moreover, the influx of foreign capital during certain periods has been an additional factor that further contributes to the appreciation of the exchange rate, thus creating an adverse effect on export performance.

Exchange rate appreciation was an obstacle to export growth in Mexico before December 1994 and in Brazil up to early 1999. It also explains the decrease in the growth rate of nontraditional exports from Chile. At the same time, Michael Bleany (1999) showed that although trade reform in Latin American countries has been successful in improving the transmission of the prices in world markets to exporters, some of the effects of the reforms have been masked by the appreciation of the exchange rate. This has depressed the profitability of exports, thus dampening export performance. In sum, the exchange rate policy in most Latin American countries in recent years has not encouraged export growth.

This does not imply, however, that appreciation is a harmful thing and that a sharp currency devaluation is desirable. In fact, a certain degree of appreciation of the exchange rate is to be expected as productivity increases and export performance improves. Furthermore, the appreciation of the exchange rate induces productivity gains by forcing companies to upgrade to better face import competition. It also allows firms to buy relatively cheaper imported equipment and inputs. Moreover, in certain circumstances it may encourage exporters to progressively move toward exporting goods with higher value added.

The tendency to a significant exchange rate appreciation in the majority of the Latin American countries may change as the region undergoes the repercussions of the financial turbulence in Asia. A certain degree of devaluation would be useful for encouraging export growth. Sharp devaluations, however, would not contribute to improving the region's capability for exporting manufactured goods.[6]

In fact, if a country's currency undergoes a significant devaluation, it may be that this will only help boost exports in the short run. In the long run, a strongly devaluated exchange rate may have a negative effect on manufactured exports because the rate would raise the price of imported inputs and equipment and isolate domestic producers from import competition. Besides, such a rate would increase the difficulties for obtaining export credit, and could foster turmoil in the domestic market—the complement of the export market for many export companies—and curtail the availability of credit for the private sector in general. Sharp devaluations generate uncertainty, thus cutting investment in productive activities. All these reasons imply that sharp devaluations are not desirable. The bursts of export growth that have been observed after sharp devaluations are usually made up of goods manufactured for the domestic market that must be exported due to the plummeting of domestic demand.

The opposite of a policy aimed at appreciating the exchange rate is not to sharply devaluate the national currency. On the contrary, it is a set of policies that allows the exchange rate to be stable in the long run, while appreciating slightly as productivity increases and the country improves its export performance. What exporters need is an exchange rate that is predictable in the long run and that at the same time encourages investment in industries manufacturing tradables.

* * *

The country studies and the policy presented in the following chapters do not cover all the issues that are essential for analyzing policies to encourage export growth. Appropriate policies for attracting foreign investment in leading manufacturing industries, for example, play an important role in promoting export growth. Likewise, the differences among rules regarding export-processing zones explain why some countries have successfully increased exports while others have lagged (Willmore 1996). At the same time, some countries have been able to attract high-technology industries to these zones (Buitelaar, Padilla, and Urrutia 1999). Economic geography explains why export companies prefer to invest in certain locations. Although these issues are critical for export performance, they are beyond the scope of this volume.

Notes

1. Baumann (1994); Bielschowsky (1994); Castillo, Dini, and Maggi (1994); Katz and Burachik (1997).

2. Policies regarding foreign direct investment and in-bond processing plants or *maquilas* are not addressed here because they are beyond the scope of the book. Nevertheless, the importance of these policies for export growth must be acknowledged, particularly in the case of Mexico.

3. The foundation for the learning by doing models of the 1980s and the 1990s is from the early 1960s: Kenneth Arrow's seminal paper (1962) has a model in which knowledge is endogenous to the production function. His model emphasizes the importance of learning, "the product of experience."

4. Further research is required to establish whether these companies did invest significant sums for expanding export capacity at a later date.

5. See Chapter 6 for a presentation of policy recommendations for increasing exports.

6. See Manuel Agosín (1993a) for a discussion of the negative impact that sharp fluctuations of the exchange rate have on export performance.

2

Mexico: Export Promotion Policies on the Cutting Edge

Adriaan ten Kate, Carla Macario, and Gunnar Niels

Mexico has been very successful at increasing exports. However, the country's greatest accomplishment has been the remarkable increase of manufactured goods exported. This performance is to a great extent the product of the decisions by transnational corporations (TNCs) to locate plants in Mexico and the effects of the North American Free Trade Agreement (NAFTA). Nevertheless, it is also the result of the country's efficient export promotion policies. This chapter sets forth Mexico's trade policies, emphasizing the government's export promotion instruments. It also presents the main features of firms' export behavior, based on a study of successful export-manufacturing companies that was carried out with the goal of deriving policy implications.

The Macroeconomic Environment

Mexico's gross domestic product (GDP) was US$428 billion in 1998, (at 1995 prices), the second highest of the Latin American and Caribbean countries, after Brazil. GDP growth rate was 4.9% for 1998, after the record growth of 6.8% for 1997 (see Table 2.1 for indicators that describe the economy's performance during the 1990s).[1]

Manufacturing's share of GDP was 20.6% in 1997, a slight increase from 18.6% in 1980 and 19.0% in 1990. Manufacturing GDP's growth rate was 10.9% in 1996 and 9.8% in 1997, after a drop of 4.9% the previous year.

Mexico has transformed its economy over the past decade by opening it up to trade and investment flows. Imports of goods and services were 33.7% of GDP in 1998, up from 17.3% in 1980. Import ratios had

Table 2.1 Mexico: Economic Indicators

	1990	1991	1992	1993	1994	1995	1996	1997	1998[g]
GDP[a]	336,713	350,792	363,680	370,020	387,144	363,234	382,074	408,140	428,077
GDP growth rates[b]	5.1	4.2	3.7	1.7	4.6	–6.2	5.2	6.8	4.9
Imports[a,c]	60,666	71,603	82,852	86,796	100,681	82,168	102,218	125,957	144,419
Exports[a,c]	49,885	56,462	59,808	66,554	76,260	89,322	107,024	125,013	137,823
Import ratio[d]	18.0	20.4	22.8	23.5	26.0	22.6	26.8	30.9	33.7
Export ratio (all goods)[d]	14.8	16.1	16.4	18.0	19.7	24.6	28.0	30.6	32.2
Export ratio (manufactures)[e]	43.3	50.8	71.1	74.6	77.3	77.5	78.1	80.7	85.1
Exchange rate[f]	2.81	3.02	3.10	3.12	3.38	6.42	7.60	7.92	9.14

Source: ECLAC, on the basis of official figures.
a. Millions of U.S. dollars at 1995 prices.
b. Average annual rates at 1995 prices.
c. Goods and services including goods for processing (*maquila*).
d. Percentages of GDP at 1995 prices. Includes goods and services.
e. Percentages of total value of FOB exports of goods. Includes goods for processing (*maquila*).
f. Nominal exchange rate in pesos per dollar.
g. Preliminary figures.
Information is from different sources, so there may be discrepancies.

been growing steadily, particularly since import liberalization in the mid-1980s (see below). Exports of goods in 1998 were US$138 billion (at constant 1995 prices), up from US$11 billion in 1980 and US$23 billion in 1985. Exports of goods and services were 32.2% of GDP in 1998, up from 10.3% in 1980. Mexico was by far the largest exporter in Latin America in 1998, while Brazil, with total exports amounting to US$62 billion was a distant second.

Consequently, Mexico's degree of openness, expressed as the sum of exports and imports of goods and services over GDP, has had a significant increase from 27.6% in 1980 and 32.8% in 1990 to 65.9% in 1998. As a point of comparison, Latin America's degree of openness for this last year is 39.6%.

However, an even more significant change has been Mexico's increased specialization in export manufactured goods, including those of the *maquiladora* industry (the in-bond processing manufacturing process). These manufacturing exports amount to 85.1% of the FOB value of total exports of goods in 1998. These numbers would certainly not be as high if the *maquila* exports were excluded, but the increased importance of manufactured products in Mexico's exports is an impressive transformation of the country's export behavior. It is also a contrast with the other countries of the region, most of which are still mainly primary goods exporters.

Hence, Mexico's export structure today is strikingly different from that of 1980, when crude oil accounted for 60.9% of exports and most other leading export products were primary agricultural or mining goods. While the main export product in 1997, including *maquila,* still is crude oil (9.4% of total exports), the next nine leading export items are all manufactured goods, such as passenger motor vehicles (8.8%), insulated wire and cable (4.5%), vans and trucks (3.6%), television sets (3.5%) and other products with high technological content such as electronic machinery or motor vehicle parts.

The surge of manufactured exports is partly due to the transformations that have taken place in the Mexican economy after import protection was substantially cut during the mid-1980s (Kate 1998). However, trade liberalization is not the only explanation, since many other countries in the region have liberalized trade in the same period without reaching similar results. Ros (1994) points out that Mexico's current industrial structure is the result of the successful import substitution development strategies of earlier decades that allowed the country to modify its comparative advantage pattern in favor of manufacturing.

The expansion of the manufacturing industries that arose from import substitution policies, together with Mexico's location advantages, attracted many TNCs, which decided to set up plants in Mexico. This in turn contributed to the increase of manufactured exports, particularly for the automotive industry. Import liberalization since 1985, and especially the enactment of NAFTA in 1994, also played a major role in TNCs' decisions to localize their production in Mexico.

Another contributing factor to Mexico's export success is that the country's firms deliberately decided to increase their exports, given the incentives provided by import liberalization and export promotion policies as well as investment in human capital and infrastructure (Máttar 1996).

At the same time, the shock to the Mexican economy as a result of the strong devaluation in December 1994 (see Table 2.1) and the ensuing plummeting of domestic demand also was a key factor in increasing the level of exports during the past years.

However, even though export performance has been impressive, it is nonetheless true that exports are highly limited to a few products, a small number of firms, and a few markets. (The most important export products are listed above.) As for the limit to firms, it should be noted that in 1995 there were slightly over 1,900 Mexican firms that exported more than US$1 million, but only about 300 of these realized more than 80% of all exports.[2] At the same time, around 85% of Mexican exports go to the United States (see Table 2.2 on page 26).

The challenge now facing the country's manufacturing industry is to attain higher output and export growth rates (Máttar and Peres 1997). Learning more about the strategies of successful Mexican exporters of manufactured goods and about the effectiveness of export promotion policies will therefore provide a useful basis from which to draw policy conclusions. These findings should prove relevant not only for Mexico but to other Latin American countries as well, since Mexico is the country in the region with the best export performance in terms of manufactured goods.

Trade Policy

Mexico followed an import substitution industrialization model since the late 1940s. Its main components were high tariffs and benchmark prices used as references by customs. There were also import licenses that varied over the years but that in some periods covered most items produced domestically.

During the 1980s, there was a radical change in the trade policy as the Mexican government proceeded to liberalize imports. This shift in focus began with the debt crisis of 1982 and was followed up by more significant changes from 1985 to 1987. During this same period, the country decided to apply for membership in the General Agreement on Tariffs and Trade (GATT), becoming a member of GATT in 1986.

As a result of these changes in trade policy, import license requirements that covered almost 100% of the domestic production in 1982 went down to 25.4% of production by December 1987, and then continued dropping, at a slower rate, to 16.5% in 1993. Tariffs were also dropped in different stages, reaching the range of 0 to 20% ad valorem by 1987, whereas before the maximum tariff had been 100% (Kate 1998). The weighted average tariff is presently below 10% ad valorem (Máttar 1998).

The country has also expanded trade by negotiating preferential trade agreements (PTAs). The most important one is NAFTA with the United States and Canada, which took effect in January 1994. NAFTA provides for a complete elimination of all tariff barriers to trade in goods in the region within 15 years, as well as for the partial elimination of many barriers to trade in services and to cross-border investment. Other trade agreements have been signed with Chile (1992), Bolivia (1995), Costa Rica (1995), the Group of Three (i.e., Colombia and Venezuela [1995]), and Nicaragua (1998). Negotiations with other Latin American countries, Israel, and the European Union are on their way. The agreement with Chile eliminated all bilateral import tariffs as of the beginning of 1998. Bolivia agreed to liberate 97% of Mexican exports from tariffs immediately. Under the agreements with Costa Rica and the Group of Three, all import tariffs will be abolished by the year 2004 (for Costa Rica trade in agriculture is not included). Nicaragua will liberate all Mexican industrial exports by 2008.

Overall, Mexico's trade balance with the countries with which it has signed trade agreements has gone from a deficit of US$2.7 billion in 1993 to a surplus of US$13.4 billion in 1997.[3] It should be noted, however, that this change in the trade balance probably has more to do with the strong devaluation of the peso in December 1994 (see Table 2.1) than with the agreements proper. A quick look at data of Mexican exports to its trade partners in Table 2.2 gives an idea about the importance of each of the trade agreements individually. As can be seen, exports to the United States, by far the largest trading partner, have increased 21.8% per year since NAFTA. Trade with Canada has grown more slowly, and the country's share in total Mexican exports has curi-

Table 2.2 Mexico's Exports (and Share of Total) to Partner Countries in Preferential Trade Agreements, Millions of U.S. Dollars at Current Prices

Partner Country	1991	1992	1993	1994	1995	1996	1997	Year of PTA	Compound annual growth of exports[a]
Chile	124	153	200	261	492	688	842	1992	37.6%
	0.30%	0.33%	0.39%	0.43%	0.63%	0.72%	0.76%		
United States	32,818	37,514	42,851	50,998	66,617	80,344	94,185	1994	21.8%
	79.62%	81.08%	82.67 %	84.22%	85.32%	83.86%	85.44%		
Canada	568	801	1,569	1,534	1,983	2,170	2,156	1994	8.3%
	1.38%	1.73%	3.03%	2.53%	2.54%	2.27%	1.96%		
Costa Rica	81	110	100	99	140	188	221	1995	30.7%
	0.20 %	0.24%	0.19%	0.16%	0.18%	0.20%	0.20%		
Colombia	152	218	239	319	459	438	513	1995	17.1%
	0.37%	0.47%	0.46%	0.53%	0.59%	0.46%	0.47%		
Venezuela	121	197	228	229	382	424	675	1995	43.4%
	0.29%	0.43%	0.44%	0.38%	0.49%	0.44%	0.61%		
Bolivia	12	8	17	11	25	30	32	1995	43.3%
	0.03%	0.02%	0.03%	0.02%	0.03%	0.03%	0.03%		
Nicaragua	17	18	21	22	32	53	64	1998	—
	0.04%	0.04%	0.04%	0.04%	0.04%	0.05%	0.06%		
Total exports	41,219	46,267	51,832	60,554	78,077	95,801	110,237	—	—

Source: ECLAC (1998a).
a. From the year before PTA to 1997.

ously decreased with respect to the last year before NAFTA (from 3.03% in 1993 to 1.96% in 1997). Overall tariff levels in these countries were already relatively low before 1994, however, and NAFTA has arguably been more important for reducing certain nontariff barriers to trade and investment.

Tariff barriers in Latin American countries tend to be much higher than those in the United States, and the agreements on tariff reductions with these countries are therefore more likely to produce significant effects on trade. This has proved especially true for the agreements with Chile, Venezuela, and Bolivia. As can be observed from Table 2.2, Mexican exports to Chile have increased almost sevenfold from US$124 million in 1991 to US$842 million in 1997. Exports to Venezuela and Bolivia increased over 43% on average per year in the first three years of the agreement. For Costa Rica, this was slightly more then 30%. Exports to Colombia have grown as well but at a slower rate. Evidence from the investigation presented below suggests that this may be due to remaining nontariff barriers to trade in this country.

Export Promotion Policies

This section describes Mexico's most important export promotion instruments. It also presents BANCOMEXT, the country's export promotion bank.[4]

Programs to Provide Access to Competitive Inputs

Mexico has several policy instruments to allow export firms to have access to a wide range of raw materials and intermediate inputs, markedly imported ones. These programs have been an important factor in the country's export growth. Although many nations have similar schemes, Mexico has been particularly successful at using them effectively and at allowing them to evolve over the years with a remarkable degree of administrative flexibility, particularly when compared with other Latin American countries. Most of these programs are run by the Ministry of Trade and Industry, while the Ministry of Finance is responsible for refunding the tax credits provided under these schemes. This section presents the main programs the country has for allowing companies to have access to competitive inputs.

The first of these schemes is the one that has encouraged the opening up of plants along the border inside in-bond processing zones, better known as the *maquiladora* regime. The *maquila* program originally allowed firms located inside in-bond processing zones to have free access to imported raw materials and, more important, components to be assembled in the plants and then shipped back to the United States. The program has existed for several decades and is mainly used by firms located in the north of the country near the border with the United States.

However, since 1989 the program is no longer restricted to a specific geographic area, and there are now plants operating under the maquila regime in other regions of the country as well. Still, plants do tend to prefer locations in the states of northern Mexico where they are closer to the border. Firms operating under this scheme can also sell a portion of their output on the domestic market. It may be stated that the maquila program has been very successful. At present, there are more than 3,100 maquiladora plants. Maquila exports increased by 20% per year between 1982 and 1995. In that last year, 39.2% of Mexico's total exports came from these processing zones, compared with only 12.0% in 1982 (ECLAC 1998a).[5]

Another instrument used by firms that are not operating under the maquila regime is the drawback. Through this instrument companies can recover the amount spent on tariffs on imported inputs used to manufacture exports. This is a typical kind of scheme used in many countries to offset an antiexport bias. In Mexico it is used mainly by firms that are occasional exporters. Firms that are regular exporters tend to prefer the Programa de Importación Temporal para Producir Artículos de Exportación (PITEX) scheme described below. Exports under the drawback scheme were US$517 million in 1995, 0.6% of the country's exports.[6]

PITEX allows exporters to import inputs on a temporary basis without paying taxes on them. The advantage of PITEX over the drawback is that it allows firms exemption not only from tariffs, but also from the value-added tax and any antidumping duties that might apply. Furthermore, there is a substantial reduction in the cost incurred by firms since there is an ex ante exemption rather than an ex post recovering of taxes—the latter being the case with drawbacks—and because fewer administrative formalities are required.

To be accepted in the PITEX, a firm must export at least US$500,000 a year or a certain percentage of its output (between 10% and 30%, according to whether the imported goods are raw materials or capital goods). The importance of the PITEX program is almost comparable to that of the maquila program. There are currently about 3,200 firms in PITEX, whose exports in 1995 were 29.3% of the country's overall exports.[7]

The program of Empresas Altamente Exportadoras (ALTEX) is a program that enables firms recognized as regularly exporting significant amounts to carry out only simplified import and export formalities, as well as quickly recover the ad valorem tax on domestic inputs used for manufacturing exports. The program has been in place since 1990. To qualify as ALTEX companies, firms must export over US$2 million or between 40% and 50% of their sales. Exports by firms included in the ALTEX scheme have amounted to approximately 7% of total exports in 1995.[8]

These export promotion programs have been very useful for export firms. They do, however, have the disadvantage of failing to provide incentives for domestic companies to become suppliers to exporters, since the programs' benefits go directly to firms that are themselves exporters. To compensate for this, changes were introduced in July 1995 with the goal of fostering linkages between export firms and the rest of the economy by providing incentives for indirect exporters.

The new rules allow firms included in programs such as ALTEX, PITEX, or the maquila system to issue "export vouchers" (*constancias de exportación*) to domestic input suppliers when the inputs are used for manufacturing exports. These vouchers enable suppliers to export companies to be exempted from paying the value-added tax on the inputs they sell to exporters, as if they were exporters themselves.

This incentive, an interesting policy innovation in the region, makes it possible to offset what was formerly an antiexport bias: export firms did not have to pay the ad valorem tax when importing inputs (since they qualified as PITEX firms, for example), but did pay it when purchasing inputs domestically. It was possible for these export firms to recover the value-added tax, but the present system is simpler and faster because it turns a tax refund into a tax exemption. Another interesting feature present in the innovation is that the private firm in the PITEX, ALTEX, or maquila program is the one issuing the voucher, so that bureaucratic formalities are reduced.

BANCOMEXT

The main goal of the Banco Nacional de Comercio Exterior (BANCOMEXT), Mexico's foreign trade bank, is to provide export financing. The bank also provides exporters with information about foreign markets, such as on tariffs and nontariff barriers, as well as about rules of origin and the specific terms of trade agreements signed by the country. In addition, BANCOMEXT administers financial and logistical support programs for firms participating in trade fairs.

BANCOMEXT's representatives in the bank's offices abroad write reports on export opportunities in specific markets. These trade commissioners also provide information for individual companies and for trade missions.

With respect to export financing, the bank operated essentially as a "second-floor" financial institution up to the mid-1990s. This means that it provided funds to the commercial banks that dealt directly with firms requiring export credit.

Nevertheless, BANCOMEXT has started operating also as a first-floor financial institution in recent years. It allocates some of its funds directly to companies with the purpose of being more active in placing export-financing funds and as a way of providing export credit to firms that have difficulties in getting access to financing through commercial banks. For instance, when the bank granted loans for US$6,316 million dollars in 1996, 22% of those funds were given directly to firms through first-floor operations (BANCOMEXT 1996).

The institution has recently had difficulties in placing all the funds it has programmed. This is because its lending rates rose after the recession that began in December 1994, as international lenders increased the country's risk premium. A small number of large export companies can often obtain lower rates abroad, but most firms in Mexico do not have access to foreign capital markets and must rely upon BANCOMEXT or domestic commercial banks. As of mid-1998, BANCOMEXT was offering export firms loans at an average rate of Libor plus 1 to 4 percentage points for loans in national currency and Libor plus 2 to 6 percentage points for loans in foreign currency.[9] These rates are much lower than those being offered by other banks in the country.

In 1996, 86.5% of all firms that received financial assistance were small and medium-sized firms (BANCOMEXT 1996). During 1997, BANCOMEXT provided financial and nonfinancial assistance to 8,289 firms. Of the 4,506 firms that received financing, 813 got it directly from the bank and 2,692 through a commercial bank. The other firms that benefited from financial assistance used programs to grant collateral that enabled them to obtain loans.[10]

Changes After NAFTA and the Uruguay Round

Since NAFTA provides for substantial cuts in most tariffs between Mexico and its main trade partner, the United States, some of the programs will become less relevant as the different stages of the trade agreement are enacted. For example, by 2001, the maquila firms will be able to sell as much as they want on the domestic market after, of course, paying the corresponding tariffs, if any.

Similarly, some of the other programs mentioned above will be phased out for exports to Canada and the United States. They will still be available for exports to non-NAFTA countries but will undoubtedly be of much less economic significance, given the importance of the United States and Canada in terms of the country's exports.

This will entail a change in the relative importance of the various export promotion policies. Providing firms with assistance in obtaining export information and carrying out market studies abroad, support for trade fair participation and assistance with financing and insurance will become increasingly important. Therefore, the role of BANCOMEXT will be even more significant than it is today.

Finally, it must be pointed out that Mexico will not have to modify its export promotion policies in order for them to be compatible with the Uruguay Round Agreements. It is one of the few countries in Latin America and the Caribbean that already has an export promotion system that is fully compatible with the multilateral trade rules. The country's export promotion system was designed from the outset to be compatible with the multilateral trade negotiations.

Firms' Export Behavior

This section presents the main findings of a research project focusing on successful exporters of manufactures in Mexico. The twelve companies included in the study are large domestic firms that export high-value-added goods. They belong to the food-processing, chemical, and automobile parts industries. TNCs and maquiladora firms were excluded, partly to ensure comparability with the research carried out for the other country studies.[11]

The main issues addressed by the research are the following: What are the principal factors that push a firm to start exporting? Is there a learning process involved in exporting activity? Which export promotion instruments do companies use and how do they evaluate them?

What are the main export obstacles? How do preferential trade agreements (PTAs) influence firms' export opportunities?

Main Factors Affecting Firms' Export Decisions

The single most significant factor that initially triggered the Mexican firms' export efforts was trying to find new markets to compensate for a drop of demand in the domestic market. Most of the companies took the decision to export during a year in which the Mexican economy was either entering or was in the middle of a recession. Hence, recessions in the domestic economy played a significant role in encouraging firms to export.

Therefore, the need to find markets for the companies' excess capacity is what pushes these Mexican firms to export. In contrast, in the industries included in the investigation long-run economies of scale (as opposed to short-run economies obtained by full utilization of *existing* capacity) were not a significant export factor.[12] In Mexico, there are a number of industries for which the domestic market—if not in recession—is large enough to allow for production at minimally efficient scales.[13]

Nonetheless, the interviews also showed that over time there is a growing persistence of the decision to export. Even if the firms included in the research tended to begin deploying export efforts during recessions, once they entered the foreign markets they maintained their presence abroad. This is because exporting provides firms with a predictable source of hard currency, decreases their vulnerability to fluctuations in the domestic market, and allows them to have greater learning and upgrading opportunities (see below).

This may not be representative of the export behavior of all companies, since many firms still consider exporting as a temporary option to dispose of excess capacity.[14] Notwithstanding, it shows a change in attitude of the managers of Mexico's larger companies, in the sense that their export activity will not, as before, disappear completely once domestic demand recovers.

Maintaining a presence in export markets was facilitated for the firms included in the investigation because they tend to be large companies. This allows them to have the financial capacity to maintain a presence in both the domestic and export markets, once the fixed cost of the activities required to enter foreign markets—such as trips abroad for initial contacts and trade fair participation, financing market studies, and hiring representatives—is covered. This is a significant change in the behavior of most Mexican firms.

Learning by Exporting

The project was designed to identify two different kinds of learning processes. The first type of learning process is directly related to how firms export, which includes finding out how and where to get the information needed to export the company's products. It also covers the learning process by which the firm acquires the skills it needs to carry out the steps to enable exporting. The second type of learning process is export related in the sense that it takes place when the firm is either manufacturing for export markets, including establishing contacts with clients abroad, but goes beyond the export process itself. This is a kind of learning accessible to firms because they are exporting, but that takes place in areas beyond export activity itself.

Learning to export. Most of the export managers who were interviewed began to export by traveling abroad, trying to contact clients and going to trade fairs, first as observers and later on with their own booths. The first step was to gather information about potential markets abroad and about the tariff and nontariff barriers to be overcome in order to gain access to those markets. The next step was to find out which were the most important trade fairs for their industry, as well as the more appropriate ones for the specific product the firm wished to export.

For example, while there are many trade fairs for the footwear industry, some of them are more suitable for relatively smaller firms because they mainly attract retailers who sell directly to consumers. Meanwhile, others are more appropriate for a company manufacturing a very high volume of output, since they are aimed at large firms that sell to department stores in the United States. There are also industries for which trade fairs are not important for the business transactions actually carried out, but simply because the fairs provide information about the state of the art in that particular industry and about the main competitors.

Therefore, the first issue that must be addressed when exporting is that of information, not only on trade issues, such as tariff and nontariff barriers, but also on industry-specific topics. The second one is financing market research abroad. This involves traveling to trade fairs, sometimes setting up a stand, sending samples, and, more generally, gathering information about foreign markets and making contacts.

Setting up a network in the United States is often relatively easy for Mexican entrepreneurs due to their close links with the Hispanic community of Mexican descent, as well as their own familiarity with that country. For example, in the 1960s one food-processing company started exporting in response to strong demand for its products by Mexican consumers living in the United States. The firm's managers realized that one of the reasons for their high sales in the north of Mexico was that their goods were being bought by Mexicans living in the United States, who frequently resold them on the other side of the border. This prompted them to try to export themselves.

In contrast, it was more difficult for firms trying to export for the first time to other countries, such as those in Latin America. In these countries, establishing contacts was often a trial-and-error process, which required a greater investment in trips abroad and finding out about the different commercial practices in each country, such as the credit terms and procedures that clients expect.

Hence, the first two main stages in acquiring export capabilities are obtaining information and establishing a network abroad. These stages demand that firm managers have the willingness and capability of investing in trying to build an export market. Beginning to export is expensive and hard and can be very frustrating in the short run. It requires a substantial investment of time and money, as well as persistence and flexibility. This condition is a sine qua non and must not be underestimated. It is probably what ultimately determines why one company becomes a successful exporter, but a similar one is unable to do so.

Although an executive's determination to export is a necessary condition, it is important to point out that the investment required to pioneer a new export market is suboptimal because the company will not be able to capture all the benefits of its investment. Once the company has gone to the expense of obtaining the information, traveling to trade fairs, contacting potential buyers, and exporting, it will be much easier for another firm in the same industry to target, from the outset, the same market that the pioneering company targeted after several costly steps. This is an area where there are externalities, in the sense that the first firm investing in opening up markets abroad will not be able to capture all the benefits of doing so. Other companies will also benefit from this pioneer activity.

In fact, several of the export managers interviewed in the course of the study mentioned that their firm had taken into account other companies' export success when evaluating the possibility of launching their own export efforts. They also said that it had been easier for them to choose a destination for their exports after finding out about other firms' success in a given export market. Similarly, several of the food-processing firms included in the survey were encouraged to export to European countries by the success that U.S. firms, such as Fiesta and El Paso, had in exporting "Tex-Mex" food products.

It must be pointed out that there are differences between industries with respect to the importance of marketing efforts abroad. While there are some industries in which they are crucial, such as the food-processing industry, there are others in which the important point is to establish contact with brokers dealing with their products. Once that is done satisfactorily, the export manager's primary concern no longer is to maintain a visible presence at trade fairs but rather to set up an export's logistics. There was a striking contrast between the export managers interviewed in consumer products manufacturing industries, who were actively looking for new markets and were in close touch with changes occurring in those markets, and those in charge of exporting commodities, such as intermediate petrochemicals, who in fact would more appropriately be "export logistics" managers.

For example, the export manager of one of the food-processing firms had spent a considerable amount of time not only going to the related trade fairs in the United States, but also getting information about the new products that were coming out in the "ethnic foods market." The firm's initial strategy for increasing exports to the United States had been to target communities with a high percentage of consumers of Mexican descent. However, the following step was to target a higher income level group, particularly the baby-boom generation that had shown its willingness to try out new food products. In this market, the Mexican firm was competing for market share with Jamaican firms that had introduced a wide variety of new products in the U.S. market. These products had many of the packaging features that are in high demand with consumers in the U.S. market, such as good-quality glass containers and colorful labels. Therefore, to preserve market share the export manager had to systematically monitor the innovations introduced by these rival firms.

By contrast, an export manager of a chemical firm was not concerned with getting new clients or losing market share to innovating rivals. His firm had long-standing contracts with a handful of U.S. companies. The product exported by his firm was an intermediate good with clearly specified and unvarying standards. Therefore, his responsibility was making sure that the transportation arrangements from the Mexican plant to destinations in the United States were adequate and timely, so that deliveries were made by deadline. This implied ensuring that the trucks got to the border at a time when the customs officers were present on both sides of the frontier and making arrangements for trucks based north of the border to transport the goods inside the United States. He had no need to be continuously informed about changes in the export market.

These differences are not irrelevant for policy purposes. They should be known to civil servants working in this area, in the sense that the support needed by different types of firms is not the same. Export promotion institutions must be aware that the kind of export assistance provided for export firms has to be adapted to the industries considered.

In sum, beginning to export involves a significant learning process: export managers, particularly those exporting goods other than commodities, have to do an in-depth search for potential markets, find out which products are in demand, manage to get into distribution channels (sometimes a very difficult feat), participate in trade fairs, and persuade clients that they have supply capabilities. Then, when they finally get an order, they hope that the client will make new orders and not jump to a cheaper supplier at the smallest variation of the exchange rate.

Therefore, government provision of export information is very useful for companies beginning to export. There are two additional reasons that stress the importance of support in this area: first, the firm cannot always completely appropriate the information it has obtained, since the mere fact that it is shipping goods abroad provides a signal to other companies; second, this kind of information—for example, about tariff and nontariff barriers in a given country—can be useful to many firms simultaneously. These are additional justifications for providing export information.

Learning from exporting. The study demonstrated that exporting also provides companies with learning opportunities in such areas as product characteristics, quality assurance, and marketing. Moreover, it enables firms to stand up to import competition in the domestic market more successfully. Over half of the managers interviewed in Mexico mentioned areas in which exporting had prompted them to upgrade the quality of their products and allowed them to know what the standards were, as well as how to meet them.

For example, one of the food-processing firms had to change the jars and the labels it used for its products. It also modified some steps of the production process, particularly those related to quality control requirements, to meet the U.S. Food and Drug Administration's (FDA) standards for imported products. These changes were initially introduced only for products manufactured for export markets, but before long they were applied to all the firm's output, hence upgrading quality for the domestic market too. Other companies in the food-processing industry had similar stories of modifying their production process to enable export and then introducing the changes in all production lines.

The reasons for extending the changes to cover all output, not only that for export markets, are twofold: (a) it has become too costly to have different standards for export products than for domestic market products; (b) many firms realized that introducing these changes allowed them to recover part of their domestic market share, which had been lost to import competition.

Selling to countries with stringent requirements, such as the United States and Japan, is particularly useful for learning while exporting. In the case of the food-processing firms, the FDA played an important role in allowing firms to upgrade the quality of their products. The fact that the FDA standards are clearly defined is very helpful. This is an important contrast to many Latin American countries' sanitary requirements that are perceived in fact as nontariff barriers.

Export-based learning also takes place in companies in industries other than food processing and in countries other than the United States. One of the chemical companies included in the study started exporting in the early 1980s, when Mexico put forth its first big manufactured-products export drive by setting up export-oriented industrial complexes. The firm's export manager believed that even though Japanese clients were difficult and demanding, they provided a valuable learning opportunity.

Similarly, a company that manufactures after-market radiator hoses improved the quality of all its output after entering export markets. The firm's chief executive officer (CEO) went through considerable efforts to try to export to Central America. In so doing, he realized that the quality of his products did not satisfy international standards. He hired a chemist to assist him in progressively adapting the quality of his inputs to meet those requirements, and today all his output conforms to international standards. This in turn has allowed his products to gain market share in Mexico itself. Meanwhile, the demands of the export process have forced him to perfect his distribution system, a learning that also has had positive spillovers in his domestic distribution system.

It can therefore be concluded that exporting does provide significant learning opportunities for the firms involved in the process, and not just in areas directly related to the export process.

While direct exporting appears to provide important learning opportunities for manufacturing firms, the same can be said for indirect exporters, that is, the suppliers to export companies that are at the cutting edge in their industry.

For instance, one firm that manufactures engine bearings and bushings for automotive assembly plants in Mexico has received several quality awards, such as Q-1 from Ford and similar ones from Nissan. Being recognized as a top-quality supplier to these world-level companies has made it easier for the firm to enter export markets. The company's managers had had to go to considerable lengths to establish their presence in foreign markets and to obtain information about how business was conducted in, for example, South American countries, but they did not have to upgrade their product's quality, since it was already recognized as outstanding. From that perspective, the link between having a presence in international markets and learning for upgrading remains. However, it does not necessarily have to be by exporting directly: being an indirect exporter to an industry that is recognized as being among the best is sufficient.

It must be pointed out, however, that "learning while being an indirect exporter" will generally be restricted to those industries and countries that have top-quality products. It will probably occur more frequently in Mexico and, for some industries, in Brazil than in other Latin American countries, most of which are not manufacturing exports that satisfy international standards.

The learning process that takes place while exporting and the positive impact it has on firms' productivity is an additional factor that promotes a more permanent presence in the export markets: several CEOs mentioned that although they began to export because of the need to use excess capacity, the learning they gained while exporting is such that it encouraged them to continue to export, even when domestic demand had recovered. The economic importance of this learning process is difficult to assess with greater precision, but there is evidence that it contributes significantly to upgrading companies' presence in both export and domestic markets.

The learning process that occurs in the domestic market itself when the firm is a supplier of a world-level industry, such as the automobile industry in Mexico, allows one to take the point further: what pushes most firms to learn when exporting is the increased competition they face when they try to market abroad and the exposure to international standards. Hence, learning is stimulated by competition and exposure to the standards of top-quality products. However, in most countries in Latin America—with the exception of some industries in Mexico and Brazil—it is exporting that provides the greatest challenge. Hence, it also provides firms with greater learning and upgrading opportunities.

Export Promotion Policies: Usefulness for Export Firms

Mexico's export promotion policies provide significant support for export firms. Assistance provided by BANCOMEXT, and sometimes by SECOFI, in supplying information on foreign markets, publishing export directories with companies' references, and financing trade fair participation has been important in the initial stages for most companies. These are precisely the areas that are the most crucial for a firm just beginning to export.

For example, one of the companies in the study that began exporting with the help of BANCOMEXT started by listing its products in the institution's export roster. This allowed it to get its first export orders. Meanwhile, contacts with several of BANCOMEXT's representatives abroad led to specific export opportunities. The institution provided financing for the firm's participation in a trade fair in Cologne, Germany, and the export manager was also able to learn more about exporting in a workshop organized by BANCOMEXT.

Other corporate executives stated that BANCOMEXT's support had been very helpful in providing export financing for the working capital they needed before reaching the point of actually shipping the goods, as well as in extending credit to the purchasing firms for the first export orders. BANCOMEXT also financed companies' participation in trade fairs abroad. In some cases, the firms no longer make use of the export bank's financial support because their own export experience allows them to get export financing elsewhere. Nevertheless, the company executives believed that the institutional support had played a key role in enabling their firms to begin exporting.

Nonetheless, while providing assistance for companies that are beginning to export is important, there are significant differences between firms with respect to the relevance of export-related information and trade fair backing. These differences are industry related.

Sustained government support is particularly important for industries aimed at markets where there are frequent changes, for example, in consumers' tastes. In these industries, trade fair participation and updated market information is vital.

In contrast, for industries exporting commodities the important step is to manage to insert the firm into a network of brokers. After that, the exporting process mainly consists of setting up the export logistics. Besides, companies exporting commodities tend to be very large firms that have less need for government assistance in export matters.

BANCOMEXT's support for export financing was critical in the early 1990s when it was very difficult for Mexican firms to get credit. At that time, exporting allowed companies to get loans that they could not have obtained otherwise. For example, interviews in Mexican garment firms in 1993 showed that at that time, when credit was scarce due to a tight monetary policy, export financing was often the only source of financing available to the medium-sized firms included in the survey (Macario 1995). In that sense, providing export financing allows partial compensation for failures of financial markets in Latin American countries.

Providing financing for export is still important today, although a number of firms—mainly the larger ones—find that they can presently get financing at better rates from other financial institutions, particularly abroad, than from BANCOMEXT. This is due to the sharp increase in rates at which BANCOMEXT has been able to get funds abroad since December 1994. This rate increase was transferred to the loans the export bank makes in Mexico, since it does not subsidize interest rates. On the other hand, rates for export financing are still very attractive for many small and medium-sized firms.

In respect to export promotion instruments for companies already exporting, such as the drawback, ALTEX, and PITEX programs discussed earlier, these are widely used by Mexican firms.[15] The few firms not using one of these programs were either barely beginning to export or did not use enough imported inputs to make it worthwhile.

In sum, Mexico's export promotion policies are efficient and supportive of firms' export efforts.

Main Obstacles to Export

The firms' executives found that there are no significant export obstacles in Mexico for exporting to the United States and Canada. While some entrepreneurs still criticize export red tape in Mexico, which obviously discriminates against smaller firms, there is a consensus about the fact that it has been considerably reduced and does not represent an important obstacle. Transportation to the United States also appears to be operating quite well. There are complaints about how ports operate and regarding railroad transportation, but there is a belief that there have been improvements.

Exporting to countries outside NAFTA does present more obstacles. These export obstacles include red tape requirements in importing countries, inadequate infrastructure, irregular shipment schedules, and difficulty in consolidating shipments. These obstacles appear to be more acute in the case of Central America: in some cases, it is cheaper and faster to ship goods from Mexico to Chile.

Bureaucratic constraints in the countries that buy Mexican exports, particularly those in Latin America, can turn into nontariff trade barriers. Venezuela, for example, requires that a government agency must issue a quality certification for every shipment of after-market automobile parts, even when the export firm is certified as a supplier to large automotive companies in Mexico and the United States. This occurs in spite of the preferential trade agreement signed by that country with Mexico and Colombia. Certificates of origin often appear to function as a similar sort of administrative nontariff trade barrier in several Latin American countries.[16]

Transporting export goods to countries outside North America also seems to be quite difficult. Mexico's roads and, in general all the country's transportation systems, are set up for exporting to the United States. This is reasonable since it is Mexico's main trading partner. However, it complicates matters for firms trying to export to other regions, as many have tried to do since the December 1994 devaluation and the subsequent recession.

Export managers also complained about the insufficient shipment frequency and the difficulties for consolidating loads. It is quite possible that these obstacles will decrease as the export of goods to other countries, such as those in Latin America, continues growing. Still, they do represent a stumbling block for companies trying to export at present.

The Influence of Preferential Trade Agreements on Firms' Export Opportunities

The aggregate data presented earlier shows that the PTAs signed by Mexico since 1992 have had a positive effect on exports. This was corroborated by the experience of the firms included in the survey. Of the twelve firms included in the research, ten said they have benefited from these PTAs. One of the two companies that had not benefited from the trade negotiations was a firm that already was exporting auto parts to the United States before NAFTA was signed and still faced a tariff that did not change much. The other firm's main export market was Central America, where it continued to face many barriers.

The impact of the preferential trade agreements on the firms included in the study can be summarized as follows. In the first place, several companies have benefited from having access to cheaper inputs because tariffs for U.S. products in Mexico have dropped. For instance, one of the companies (an orange juice manufacturer) saw the tariff on several inputs not produced domestically drop to 0%. Meanwhile, its market in Chile grew substantially because the tariff imposed upon its product was also abolished.

Another example is a polyester manufacturer that benefited from NAFTA: production was located in Mexico, precisely due to that PTA. Meanwhile, the company's market share in Chile also increased considerably because it replaced other input sources in that country. Similarly, one auto parts firm was able to continue selling in Venezuela, in spite of the recession in that country, due to the preferences negotiated in the Group of Three (G-3) PTA among Colombia, Mexico, and Venezuela.[17]

Of these trade negotiations, the one that has had the strongest impact is of course NAFTA with the United States and Canada. This agreement has not only expanded the companies' export opportunities but also allowed them to have access to less expensive or higher quality inputs, thus contributing to the enhancement of the firms' productivity.

Nevertheless, as discussed above, other PTAs signed by Mexico in the early 1990s also have had beneficial effects, particularly because tariff levels in Latin America tend to be (before trade negotiations) quite high, much higher than those of the United States. Therefore, the marginal effect of these agreements on the decrease of tariffs can be quite significant.

In spite of the overall increase in exports to the G-3, the firms included in the research complained that Colombia and Venezuela, even after signing the trade agreement, have a series of nontariff trade barriers that were not included in the negotiations but that remain important obstacles to increases in trade. An example of these barriers is the need to prove compliance with sanitary conditions or carrying out long and cumbersome formalities for each shipment.

In the longer run, in addition to increased trade, the entrepreneurs interviewed believe that the PTAs will have another positive effect through their impact on firms' investment decisions, most particularly, locational ones. For example, they are clearly aware that NAFTA has played an important role in the decisions of several transnational companies to set up or revamp their plants in Mexico. Similarly, the investments by Mexican firms in Chile in such industries as food processing, where Bimbo bought Ideal, and in the infrastructure, where Bufete Industrial bought Ovalle Moore, were strongly influenced by the PTA between the two countries.

The fact that PTAs have had a significant impact on companies' export opportunities suggests that a great deal of care has to be taken when negotiating them so as to ensure consideration of such aspects as the importance of trade diversion and of strategic decisions about which countries will be the major trade partners. It appears that these points were expressly taken into account when negotiating the trade agreements Mexico signed in the early 1990s. Nevertheless, another feature that should be taken into account in the course of the negotiations is that the agreement really does increase trade opportunities and that trade will not be hindered by nontariff barriers.

Conclusions

The project found that the main motivation for companies to begin exporting was the need to offset the fall of demand in the domestic market. Thus, it was the need to find markets for output that could no longer be sold in the domestic market that drove these firms to export. In contrast, economies of scale have not been a factor that stimulated export activity for the companies included in the survey.

These firms' presence in export markets is also, however, taking on a more permanent nature. This new trend takes hold as corporate executives (once they have started to export) cease viewing export markets as a temporary outlet for excess capacity, but instead come to regard them as a permanent complement to the firms' domestic market share. Exporting allows firms a reliable source of hard currency and decreases vulnerability to the fluctuations of the domestic market. It also provides companies with learning and upgrading opportunities.

To begin exporting, companies have to obtain information and establish a network abroad. It was easier for Mexican entrepreneurs to start exporting to the United States than to other markets, such as those of Latin American countries.

Several of the executives in the study made the decision to begin exporting after witnessing the success of another export firm in the same industry. This shows that a firm's success in selling to a new market abroad rapidly provides a signal to other companies in the same industry. Furthermore, the information on tariff and nontariff barriers obtained by one firm can be useful for another company in the same industry. A firm that is a successful pioneer exporter bears greater costs than the companies that follow in its path. Hence, private investment in obtaining export information is suboptimal because the pioneer export company cannot appropriate all the benefits of this investment, but instead generates positive externalities that benefit latecomers. This confirms the fact that the cost of providing export information should not be borne exclusively by individual firms.

There is also evidence that support for export firms needs to be tailored to the specific industries involved. Exporting manufactured consumer goods is much more demanding than exporting commodities. Export promotion institutions should consider this when designing support programs.

Exporting—by exposing firms to competition and to demanding international standards—provides companies with considerable learning opportunities about the prevailing standards in export markets and how they should go about upgrading to satisfy these standards. There is a significant learning process that takes place within firms as they adapt their production and distribution processes to satisfy export market requirements. This process allows the acquisition of a substantial amount of knowledge that permits an outward shift of the production function. In sum, when companies start exporting they get on a steeper learning curve. The greater learning and upgrading opportunities that export activity provides to firms were found in companies that exported indirectly as well as those engaged in direct export activity. In other words, the opportunities exist for both suppliers to exporters and for exporters themselves.

This learning capability requirement, which is at the same time an obstacle for firms trying to export and an advantage for those that are successful at doing so, is crucial at a time when the pace of change in demand has accelerated. Enabling and encouraging more companies to get on such a learning curve could have significant positive effects in terms of firms' productivity. Exposing companies to competition and world-level standards in a given industry and allowing them access to the upgrading tools required to compete in such markets is probably one of the most efficient and significant kinds of support that public policy could provide, in both small and in large economies.

Mexico's export promotion programs are very useful for export firms. Companies make extensive use of the export promotion instruments available to them, such as the PITEX and ALTEX programs, as well as of the assistance provided by BANCOMEXT in the forms of export information and financing. The government's ability to set up programs that allow companies to have ready access to a wide range of inputs and to streamline bureaucratic export formalities is outstanding and sets it apart from its counterparts within the region. Moreover, these export promotion programs have the additional advantage of being fully compatible with the Uruguay Round Agreements.

BANCOMEXT provides export firms with substantial support, although it has had more difficulty since December 1994. This financial institution will become even more relevant in the coming years as some of the government's export promotion programs are partially phased out. The export bank is an exemplary institution, but it will have to adapt if it is to have the flexibility and ability to provide the kind of support firms will need to cope with the new challenges in export markets. This is important if BANCOMEXT wants to ensure its ability to continue contributing to an increase in the number of export companies.

Therefore, even though there is still room for improvement—such as a further reduction in export formalities in some programs and a greater adaptation of BANCOMEXT's programs to the evolving needs of export firms—Mexico's export promotion policies appear to be very effective. They play a particularly crucial role in the initial stages of export activity, when companies need information about how to access foreign markets and obtain financing for participation in trade fairs. They are also among the best in Latin America in terms of enabling firms to gain access to competitive inputs.

Hence, while Mexico's export success is mainly the result of a wide range of economic policies, of the size of the country's manufacturing sector, and of its proximity to the United States, the country's export promotion system also makes a valuable contribution to this export success. Complaints about the red tape required for exporting notwithstanding, export promotion programs such as PITEX and ALTEX and the support provided by BANCOMEXT help firms to export and are an important factor in the country's export success.

This policy advantage is a result of the government's determination to increase exports. It is also the product of the administrative capability Mexican export promotion institutions possess thanks to their highly qualified professionals and their flexibility in adapting programs to firms' needs. Mexican entrepreneurs often complain that the government is rigid and takes too long to change its policies. But when one compares the institutional capability of Mexican export promotion institutions with that of other such agencies in Latin American and Caribbean countries, Mexico has a clear advantage. The new incentives for indirect exporters are a good example of this. Moreover, the public sector has the capability needed to administer a number of different export facilitation schemes, such as the ALTEX and PITEX programs. By contrast, there are several Latin American and Caribbean countries that lack the administrative capability even to administer standard programs, such as a drawback scheme.

Companies do not face any significant obstacle in Mexico when exporting to the United States or Canada. Yes, some aspects of the country's infrastructure still appear to be deficient, such as its railroads and port facilities, but entrepreneurs believe that quite a bit of progress has been made in recent years and that more will be made in the near future.

On the other hand, firms face major obstacles when trying to export to Latin American countries. The main obstacles include inadequate infrastructure, irregular and costly shipment options, and red tape in the importing countries. A lack of transparency with respect to commercial practices and to national commercial legislation in these countries also hinders export opportunities. Some of these obstacles will become less of a constraint as trade expands, since this can be expected to permit an increase of shipment frequencies and to provide more opportunities for cargo consolidation. Others will have to be addressed by government-level negotiations, such as the nontariff barriers resulting from bureaucratic and procedural requirements.

Regional PTAs provide export firms with greater access not only to markets abroad, but also to a wider range of imported inputs. NAFTA, for example, has allowed the companies included in the study to increase their exports and also to obtain imported inputs at a lower cost than before the agreement went into effect. The agreements negotiated by Mexico with Latin American countries have also led to an increase in export opportunities, particularly in the case of Chile. The positive long-term locational effects of these agreements in terms of companies' decisions to set up plants in a country to benefit from these larger markets was also stressed by the entrepreneurs who were interviewed. Last, the opportunities provided by these agreements, which have opened up new markets for Mexican firms, have contributed to the country's economic recovery after the recession that was triggered in December 1994.

Notes

1. The information included in this section, unless otherwise specified, is from ECLAC (1999b) and (1999c).

2. Information provided by SECOFI.

3. Information provided by Mexico's Trade Commissioner in Chile.

4. This section is based on Kate and Niels (1996).

5. The research presented in this chapter did not cover maquila firms, since one of the criteria used was to include comparable companies in the different countries covered by the study. However, a description of this scheme is given in this section to provide a point of reference for comparing the impact of the different export promotion instruments.

6. Information provided by SECOFI.

7. Information provided by SECOFI.

8. Information provided by SECOFI.

9. Information provided by BANCOMEXT.

10. Information provided by Mexico's trade commissioner in Chile.

11. For a detailed description of the firms included in the project, the criteria for selecting them, and the main findings of the study, see Macario (1998a).

12. This outcome is different from the one obtained in the studies in Chile and Colombia. The reason for these contrasting findings is the difference in size of the countries' domestic markets. See the corresponding chapters.

13. However, there are industries in which operating at a world-level scale entails having plants whose level of output is larger than most domestic markets, including Mexico's. This is the case, for example, of some products of the petrochemical industries.

14. One of the goals of the present Mexican administration is to make that nation's firms' presence in export markets more permanent. This objective is based on the perception that many companies remain in export markets for only a short period (interview with SECOFI officials).

15. No results are given on the maquila scheme because no maquila firm was included in the study.

16. Note that although Mexican manufacturers mentioned on several occasions that obtaining certificates of origin was a cumbersome procedure, Chilean entrepreneurs claim that they are facing unfair competition from Mexican firms exporting after-market parts that are in fact not manufactured in Mexico, but in Asia. The main reason for getting away with this practice, according to the Chilean manufacturers, is the laxity of the Mexican authorities in delivering certificates of origin. Whatever the real reason for the loss of market share by the Chilean firms in question, this event shows that streamlining administrative procedures is not always that simple, and that complex negotiations may be involved.

17. These results have a strong selection bias, since this is a sample of successful exporters. The conclusions drawn here for a small number of firms do not allow one to conclude that the majority of Mexican firms have benefited from NAFTA and the other PTAs signed by Mexico in recent years. It is still too early to assess the impact of these PTAs on the Mexican manufacturing industry, and interviewing a small number of firms is in any event not the correct way to do so. However, the interviews were a good opportunity to get some preliminary information on this topic as it relates to export firms.

3

Chile: In Search of a New Export Drive

Carla Macario

Chile was a pioneer of trade reform in Latin America, particularly during the late 1970s and the early 1980s. The country was also a forerunner with respect to export promotion policies. The outcome of these reforms was that the nation successfully increased exports over the course of many years.

Yet, recent years have shown that the country needs new policies if it wants to regain the ability to have exports growing at high rates. The recent fall in exports can be partially explained by the economic turbulence that began in Asia and then spread to Latin America. Nevertheless, the fall is also due to a specialization in exporting a few natural-resource-intensive commodities that made the country vulnerable to fluctuations of the business cycle in export markets. This specialization is the result of inappropriate macroeconomic policies—from the standpoint of promoting export growth—combined with a dwindling of the efforts to introduce policy innovations leading to sustained export growth. This chapter examines Chile's policies from the perspective of promoting exports.

The Macroeconomic Environment

Chile's GDP was US$77 billion in 1998 (Table 3.1). GDP growth rate was 7.0% in 1997 and 3.1% in 1998. After more than a decade during which the country went through several recessions (in the 1970s and in the early 1980s)—and performed poorly in terms of growth rate (GDP dropped by a yearly average of 0.2% between 1980 and 1985) the economy started improving and showed steady growth. The GDP grew at an

Table 3.1 Chile: Economic Indicators

	1990	1991	1992	1993	1994	1995	1996	1997	1998[g]
GDP[a]	44,787	48,072	53,347	56,857	59,775	65,200	69,694	74,581	76,882
GDP growth rates[b]	3.3	7.3	11.0	6.6	5.1	9.1	6.9	7.0	3.1
Imports[a,c]	9,314	9,794	12,379	13,716	14,760	18,214	20,173	22,950	23,166
Exports[a,c]	11,897	12,974	14,972	15,409	17,092	19,234	21,922	24,285	25,776
Import ratio[d]	20.8	20.4	23.2	24.1	24.7	27.9	28.9	30.8	30.1
Export ratio (all goods)[d]	26.6	27.0	28.1	27.1	28.6	29.5	31.5	32.6	33.5
Export ratio (manufactures)[e]	10.9	12.7	13.2	16.1	16.4	13.2	14.3	15.2	16.9
Exchange rate[f]	305	349	363	404	420	397	412	419	460

Source: ECLAC, on the basis of official figures.
a. Millions of U.S. dollars at 1995 prices.
b. Average annual rates at 1995 prices.
c. Goods and services.
d. Percentages of GDP at 1995 prices. Includes goods and services.
e. Percentages of total value of FOB exports of goods.
f. Nominal exchange rate in pesos per U.S. dollars.
g. Preliminary figures.
Information is from different sources, so there may be discrepancies.

average yearly rate of 8.3% during the period 1991–1997 (Rosales 1999). This performance stands out in Latin America where most countries have at best been growing at rates of between 2 and 4% per year.[1]

The country's ability to grow at relatively high rates was due to the combination of several determinants, such as stable macroeconomic policies, the setting up of private pension funds that encouraged saving and investment, a reduction of the government's intervention in the economy, and a countrywide consensus of what economic policy should be. Still, one of the major factors credited with allowing this performance was the transformation of the Chilean economy from one of import substitution to one that has opened up and in which exports play a major role. Chile's degree of openness, expressed as the sum of imports and exports over GDP, was 63.6% in 1998, up from 32.2% in 1970.

The country's exports of goods and services reached US$24.3 billion in 1997 and US$25.8 billion in 1998, measured at constant 1995 prices. Exports' share of GDP has grown steadily from 12.6% in 1970 and 25.9% in 1985 to 33.5% in 1998. Export growth has been determinant for the growth of the Chilean economy (Agosín 1997; García, Meller, and Reppetto 1996). Hence, Chile has been very successful in transforming its economy from a closed one to one that has opened up substantially and in which exports play a major role (Table 3.2).

Yet, this export performance is somewhat mitigated by the fact that most of the country's exports are still primary goods. In 1997 Chile's leading ten export products were refined copper (27.9%), copper ores (12.1%), fish (5.1%), wood pulp (3.6%), meat and fish meal (3.3%), wine (2.5%), grapes (2.5%), gold (2.3%), unrefined copper (2.2%), and lumber (1.7%). Therefore, the ten main products accounted for over 63% of the country's exports, demonstrating a significant concentration of exports in a few products, of which 42% are copper based.

Table 3.2 Chile: GDP and Export Growth 1980–1997 (Percentage, average annual growth)

	GDP	Exports
1980–1985	0.06	2.24
1985–1990	6.36	11.41
1990–1995	7.18	8.62
1995–1997	6.85	9.94

Source: ECLAC, on the basis of official figures.

The share of copper products has decreased considerably since 1970, when it accounted for 78.8% of the country's exports (ECLAC 1998b). Copper is less important than in the past, but it is still very important for the trade balance and even more so for the public sector's budget. The weight of copper in the country's exports implies that the economy is very sensitive to the fluctuations of the price of copper on world markets. The same can be said of meals and wood pulp, although to a lesser extent.

For instance, the fall of the prices of the country's main export products led to a decrease in the export of goods from US$16.9 billion in 1997 to US$14.9 billion in 1998, measured at current market prices. While exports of goods measured in volume increased by 6.8% during this period, a fall of 17.6% of the prices of the goods exported explains the decrease of 12.0% of the value of exports of goods.

This shows that concentration in the export of a few natural-resource-intensive commodities makes the Chilean economy highly vulnerable to fluctuations in international markets. And most of the decrease is the consequence of reduced mineral exports, essentially due to the plummeting of the price of copper. Nevertheless, revenue from other export products also fell. For example, the price of wood pulp—one of the country's main exports—went down for the third year in a row.

Most of the leading exports had very low processing levels: in 1998, only 16.9% of the country's exports were manufactured products, one of the lowest percentages in the region. This hinders the incorporation of the latest technological innovations with the potential of leading to positive spillovers in the rest of the economy.

Moreover, there is a strong concentration in the number of export firms. Ten principal firms exported 40% of exports during the first semester of 1997, while 59% of the companies exported less than US$100,000 per year (ProChile 1997). This is combined with a high rate of turnover among exporters (the number of companies that export one year and do not the following year)—which reaches 35%. This means that there are many firms that export sporadically instead of on a regular basis.

There is also a significant limit to export destinations: they go to a small number of countries. In 1997 the main exports markets were the United States (15.9%), Japan (15.7%), Great Britain (6.2%), South Korea (5.8%), Brazil (5.6%), and Taiwan and Argentina (4.6% each). Therefore, almost half the country's main export markets are in only five countries.

At the same time, there has been a decrease in the annual rate of growth of nontraditional exports from 21.8% in 1995 to 6.9% in 1997 to 3.6% for 1998 (Banco Central de Chile 1999). This is clear evidence that the export diversification push has weakened over the last years.

The country's specialization in exporting a few natural-resource-intensive commodities has been reinforced by the appreciation of the exchange rate. The Chilean peso has had a sustained appreciation since the early 1990s, which was brought about by several factors. One of them was the sizable flow of capital to Latin American economies during most of the 1990s, particularly before the 1994 Tequila shock. At the same time, the significant investments in large mining projects and in forestry, paper, and pulp enterprises also contributed to the appreciation of the peso.

For example, despite the depreciation of the peso during a few months of 1997, the real exchange rate of the peso appreciated by 8.4% during that year. In fact, the rate of appreciation up to October 1997—just before the country started experiencing the effects of the economic turbulence in Asia—was 10.4% (Banco Central de Chile 1999). This compounded a sustained appreciation over several years, far higher than what could be explained by increases in productivity. The appreciation of the peso for several years contributed to a decrease in the inflation rate to 4.7% for 1998, the lowest in several decades. But such appreciation has curtailed export growth.

Exchange rate appreciation has been particularly high in relation to countries outside Latin America, since appreciation with respect to the region was somewhat mitigated by the significant appreciation of currencies in some countries, such as Brazil, up to the beginning of 1999.

Moreover, this appreciation happened at the same time as an account deficit that was already higher than 5% of GDP even before the onset of the economic troubles in Asia and the ensuing fall in the price of copper (Rosales 1999). There was a change in the trend during the second semester of 1998 that led to a 3.6% depreciation of the peso for that year (Banco Central de Chile 1999), and the same trend continued during the first months of 1999. Nonetheless, the magnitude of the depreciation certainly was not an accurate reflection of an economy that has seen the price of its main export products fall and the current account deficit continue growing to about 7% of GDP (ECLAC 1999d).

Trade Policy

Chile started transforming its economy after the military coup that overthrew Allende's government in September 1973. An import substitution development strategy that had been in place for several decades was replaced by one based on opening up the economy and emphasizing outward-oriented growth. At the same time, the government's intervention in the economy was slashed. The banks, manufacturing firms, and land that had been put under government control under Allende were privatized. The same was done with other state-owned firms in the following years. Concurrent with these changes, new policies were designed to foster the establishment of a domestic capital market (Ramos 1986).

Trade policy was radically transformed. At the end of Allende's government tariffs varied widely, from 0 to 750%, the average tariff being 94%. In addition to these high tariffs, there were various nontariff barriers, such as the prohibition on importing certain goods and the requirement to make large deposits to import other merchandise (Ffrench-Davis 1980).

The trade policy changes introduced after September 1973 were the following: nontariff barriers were almost completely eliminated, while all tariffs above 200% were cut to that level. Tariffs were then progressively reduced and the dispersion decreased, so that by 1979 a flat tariff of 10% applied to most goods. In 1980 the average tariff was 10.1% (Ffrench-Davis 1989). During that period Chile was a forerunner of trade reform in Latin America.

Nevertheless, the export push that could have been expected from trade liberalization was dampened by the appreciation of the peso, as the government started using the nominal exchange rate to control inflation. This decision—combined with the laxity of regulations in the financial system and an abundance of financial flows from the industrialized countries—contributed to making the import of goods much more profitable than manufacturing them in the country: while exports grew at annual rates of 14.4% between 1974 and 1981, imports grew at a rate of 22.5%. As a result, in 1981 Chile's current account deficit was 18% of GDP (Ffrench-Davis, Leiva, and Madrid 1992). It is not trade liberalization as such that explains these events, but rather the incompatibility between the trade policy and the exchange rate policy due to their having different goals.

In the early 1980s, there was a substantial decrease in financial flows to developing countries. In the case of Chile this was compounded by a drop in the price of copper, the country's main export good and also a significant source of revenue for the public sector. The economy went into a severe recession as GDP dropped by 15.7% in 1982. There was a devaluation, and unemployment rates increased sharply. Tariffs were raised again so that the average tariff went up gradually from 10.1% in 1982 to 25.8% in 1985.

As the economy recovered, tariff levels were again progressively reduced. The policy mix during the period 1990–1996 was successful, allowing the country to continue increasing exports and to maintain the trade deficit at a moderate level (Agosín and Ffrench-Davis 1998). Chile has consolidated tariffs with the WTO at a maximum rate of 25%, bringing it down from 35%. This relatively low rate was chosen precisely to show the country's determination to have low tariffs. The only exceptions are sugar, wheat, and oil for human consumption and oil seeds (GATT 1991; DIRECONBI 1994).

At present, one of the key elements of Chile's trade policy is a flat tariff of 10%. It was 11% for several years until January 1999, when a 1% reduction was applied. There will be a further cut of 1% per year for the next four years, reaching 6% by 2003. This is the tariff applied to imports from countries with which Chile has not negotiated PTAs, the goal of this further reduction being a decrease in the trade diversion effect of the PTAs.

The other key element of the country's trade policy is the negotiation of PTAs that have been actively pursued since the early 1990s. Chile has such agreements with Canada, Colombia, Ecuador, Mexico, Peru, and Venezuela. The country has a special trade agreement with Bolivia. Chile is an associate member of MERCOSUR, the customs union set up by Argentina, Brazil, Paraguay, and Uruguay. The country is not a full member of MERCOSUR so as to avoid the high common external tariff applied by that customs union. Chile belongs to the Asia Pacific Economic (APEC) Forum, an organization that promotes trade among countries of the Pacific Rim. As a result of the numerous preferential trade agreements, the average tariff on imports to Chile is in fact around 8% and not flat.

Export Promotion Policies

Among Chile's export promotion policies are those that are aimed at compensating the antiexport bias, the schemes that seek to encourage exports and the institutional support for export activities.[2] Information on the amount of funds used to finance the instruments or the share of exports using them is provided whenever available.

Policies to Compensate the Antiexport Bias

Drawback. This scheme, set up in 1988, allows firms to recover the tariffs paid when importing inputs used to manufacture exports. It is the standard instrument that most countries use to enable companies to compensate the antiexport bias that results from tariffs. It also lets firms have access to a wide range of inputs, particularly imported ones. It does not confer the recovery of countervailing duties nor of antidumping penalties.

The petrochemical industry has been the one to benefit the most from the drawback—43.0% of the funds spent from 1988 to 1993—along with the mining sector (26.37%) (Servicio Nacional de Aduanas 1994). Approximately US$30 million were used to finance this instrument in 1997.

That this instrument is operative in Chile provides domestic firms with an advantage over the companies in the majority of Latin American countries. Most nations in the region do not have drawback systems that function in practice even if they do theoretically exist in the legislation.

Nevertheless, even in Chile this scheme involves complex paperwork requirements, and large companies have a greater ability to comply with the requirements. By contrast, medium and small-sized firms find it more difficult to gather all the information necessary for the drawback. Up to now they have tended to prefer using the Reintegro Simplificado, an export subsidy described below.

Value-added tax refund. This system, set up in 1974, allows firms to get a refund of the value-added tax paid when buying products for export or inputs for manufacturing exports. It is a usual arrangement aimed at avoiding double taxation.

Export warehouses. The export warehouses, Almacenes Particulares de Exportación, allow firms manufacturing exports to store imported inputs or parts that will be used to make export products. Firms using these warehouses can bring the imports into the country without paying tariffs or the value-added tax. This scheme allows companies to avoid taxes for imports when storing or manufacturing exports. Hence, it differs from the two instruments described above that allow firms to recover taxes after paying them and therefore have a higher financial cost.

Export Subsidies

Simplified drawback scheme for nontraditional exports. This export promotion instrument, the Reintegro Simplificado, was set up in 1985. Its goal is to allow firms to obtain a subsidy roughly equal to the refund of tariffs on imported inputs used to manufacture nontraditional export goods. It allows exporters of nontraditional goods to get a refund of 3, 5, or 10% of the FOB value of the exports. To qualify for this refund, the firm must be exporting a product that has a maximum of 50% of imported inputs and, most important, of which total exports of that product by all companies in the country in a given period were below a specified threshold.

For example, to have the right to a refund of 10%, the total exports of a given good must have been in the previous year under US$11.6 million. For a refund of 5% the maximum threshold is set at US$17.4 million, and for 3% at US$20.9 million. Hence, as the exports of a given product (defined by its tariff item) increase and pass the thresholds, they drop to the lower refund levels—say from 5 to 3%—until they are excluded, precisely because of the export success.

This policy, innovative in Latin America, seeks to encourage the entry into markets abroad of products that had not previously been exported and to bolster export diversification. The policy has contributed to increasing the number of export firms, particularly small and medium-sized companies.

The amount spent on this instrument was US$210 million in 1996, an average of 8.7% of the value of the exports that can use it (Banco Central de Chile 1998). In 1992, 78% of the funds used for reimbursing exporters were paid under this drawback scheme (DIRECONBI 1994), and approximately 2,200 firms use it.

Firms in the food and beverage industry, and wood-processing, paper, printing, and chemical companies are the main users of this arrangement. It is an effective scheme for encouraging export diversification because it has promoted the entry of new products into export markets at a low fiscal cost. It also self-destroys in the sense that once the policy is successful—that is, once a certain export threshold has been reached for a given product—there are no longer any export subsidies for that good. It could also be used as a scheme to promote exporting to new markets, if it were slightly modified by changing the rule of total exports of a given good to one that specifies exports to a given market (Macario 1995).

Nevertheless, although it is supposed to be a tariff refund, this instrument is in fact (at least in part) an export subsidy. Even if tariffs were effectively paid on imported inputs, nothing guarantees that they were in the percentage being refunded. Therefore this scheme is not compatible with the Uruguay Round Agreements, which established that most nonagricultural export subsidies should be eliminated by the year 2003. The only exceptions allowed are export subsidies in countries belonging to the group of nations with the lowest incomes, which does not include Chile. Moreover, products benefiting from this arrangement may also be subject to countervailing measures in importing countries.

The scheme for importing capital goods. This subsidy, based on a 1987 law, allows companies to delay for up to seven years the payment of tariffs due for importing capital goods, which is then scheduled in three payments. If equipment is bought in the country instead of being imported, it allows the buyer to have a tax credit for 73.0% of the tariff that would have been applied had the good been imported, hence 7.3% for a tariff of 10.0%.

This scheme assists firms manufacturing for the domestic market, as well as exporters. Hence it is not only an export subsidy, but also a subsidy for buying equipment for manufacturing for the domestic market. The amount currently being spent on this incentive is about US$30 million per year.

However, if the capital goods imported under this policy are used to manufacture exports, then it is possible for the company to avoid paying the tariffs. To be able to do so, the firm must have exported at least 10% of its total sales in the previous two years—for the first payment—and this is to increase to 60% for the next two payments. In that sense, it favors exporters above manufacturers for the domestic market. So this subsidy is not compatible with the Uruguay Round Agreements, and it will have to be eliminated by the year 2003.

Export Financing

In addition to the main export credit programs described below, export firms have access to loans from commercial banks and to financing from the Corporación de Fomento de la Producción (CORFO), the country's development agency.

Financing for collateral for nontraditional exports. The Fondo de Garantía para Exportaciones No-Tradicionales, set up in 1987, provides export firms with up to 50% of what banks require as collateral when granting loans to finance exports. To qualify for this support, firms must be exporting a nontraditional product. The maximum is around US$200,000 per year for each exporter. This is not a direct export-financing mechanism, but rather one that allows companies to have collateral, thus facilitating access to the export financing offered by the commercial banks. Firms rarely use it. Three collateral arrangements were approved in 1995 and two in 1996 (OMC 1997a).

Financing for purchase of Chilean exports. CORFO provides borrowing facilities for foreign firms buying Chilean capital goods, consumer durables, and engineering and consulting services. This allows a company importing the goods and services credit for up to ten years, while the Chilean exporter is paid immediately.

The development agency has this sort of export line of credit with the Corporación Andina de Fomento (the development bank of the Comunidad Andina), with the Central American Integration Bank, and with banks in Argentina, Costa Rica, Mexico, and Peru. Such long-term export financing is very helpful in putting Chilean exporters on the same footing as firms from other countries that are able to offer credit to purchasers. This is typically the case of U.S. and European capital goods firms, and also of Brazilian and Mexican companies.

Export investment financing. CORFO has a long-term borrowing facility to finance export investment for Chilean export firms. This instrument is available to companies with annual sales under US$30 million. It allows firms to finance the purchase of inputs and other items used in the production process. It also covers the expenses of marketing abroad, such as setting up offices, warehouses, or retail stores outside the country. Firms can obtain loans of up to US$3 million for these purposes and repay them within eight years.

Export insurance. CORFO provides companies with assistance for export insurance through the instrument known as Cubos Exportación that subsidizes 50% of the cost of export insurance for firms with yearly sales under US$10 million. Export insurance availability has also increased somewhat thanks to programs offered by the Asociación de Exportadores de Manufacturas (ASEXMA), the exporters' trade association.

Institutional Support for Export Activities

ProChile. ProChile, the country's trade promotion organization (TPO), belongs to the Ministry of Foreign Affairs. It was created in 1975 with the goal of promoting nontraditional exports, diversifying exports, and breaking into new markets abroad. It has twelve offices in Chile and thirty-eight abroad.

The TPO's activities are presently aimed at increasing exports from the companies that are already exporting and at adding to the number of export firms. The agency has also set the goal of encouraging companies that are large exporters to be more involved in export markets through strategic alliances with foreign firms.

ProChile provides information on the formalities required for exporting, export promotion instruments, requirements for exporting to given markets, tariffs, and trade fairs abroad. It publishes several magazines with export information and an export directory. The TPO's web site has information on the country's export products and the companies manufacturing them, thus facilitating the flow of information for potential clients abroad.

The agency works closely with the private sector through small associations that organize export firms in 180 industry-based entrepreneurial groups, such as one for the wine exporters. Through these groups ProChile provides companies with assistance for marketing abroad, including designing strategies for different markets. The firms benefiting from this assistance must finance half of the expenses.

ProChile has a yearly budget of US$22 million, of which US$10 million are earmarked for agricultural products. The 2,000 export firms working with the agency, of a total of 5,000 for the country, sell around a third of Chile's exports.

In addition to its activities of the past several years, the TPO is now providing firms with financial assistance for establishing offices abroad. This new activity is to enable tighter links between export firms and their clients abroad, and to encourage companies to export on a regular basis.

The agency has played an important role in making it easier for small and medium-sized companies to try to export, hence allowing an increasing number of firms to export and a greater export diversification. It has also enabled participation in trade fairs to become a customary practice. The TPO has fostered a spirit of collaboration between government institutions and trade associations, such as ASEXMA, that is beneficial for policy success.

The effective support provided by ProChile, the streamlined export formalities, and the export subsidy for minor or emerging exports—the Reintegro Simplificado—contributed to the country's exporting products across a wide range of tariff items, particularly during the late 1980s and the early 1990s. It also explains why medium-sized firms can be exporters, in contrast to what happens in other countries in Latin America, where exporting is an activity most often carried out only by the largest companies.

Nevertheless, the demands of export firms in terms of export assistance are much more complex today than they were a decade ago. The current organizational structure of ProChile—that of a standard government agency—precludes it from having the flexibility, autonomy, and financial resources it needs to be able to respond to these demands.

Therefore, the TPO will change its legal status, if Chile's congress approves the new legislation, to that of an independent corporation. While remaining under the control of the Ministry of Foreign Affairs, the TPO's new board of directors will include delegates from the private-sector trade associations. The goal of this change is to give the institution greater flexibility and autonomy, thus allowing it to respond more quickly to the needs of export firms.

In the meantime, the agency has gradually been transferring the responsibility for some export promotion activities to the private sector, by channeling funds to trade associations, such as ASEXMA, and other organizations with which it has signed agreements.

The asociación de exportadores de manufacturas. ASEXMA is the trade association of firms exporting manufactured goods. It provides companies with information on export formalities, export promotion schemes, and markets abroad. This trade association provides information directly and through a web page, assists firms in participating in trade fairs, organizes trade missions, and organizes workshops to discuss policy issues that are critical for exporters.

The association has worked closely with ProChile in setting up groups of exporters for specific industries. These groups carry out such activities as marketing abroad, participating in trade fairs, and opening offices in countries picked as target markets.

ASEXMA and the German Agency for Technical Assistance manage a project aimed at improving the export supply capability of small and medium-sized firms. The project provides around forty export firms with technical assistance in matters related to quality, technology, entry into markets abroad, trade fair participation, and design of marketing strategies.

Firms' Export Behavior

The main features of the behavior of export manufacturing firms in Chile presented here are based on the findings of a research project, carried out in footwear and printing firms, that compared export and non-export companies. The ultimate goal of the investigation was to establish which policies would be most effective for increasing manufactured exports.[3]

The main issues addressed were the following: What are the chief determinants that push a firm to export? How do companies learn to export? Do export firms have access to greater learning opportunities that allow them to get on steeper learning curves than companies selling only in the domestic market? How useful are export promotion policies for export companies? Are there significant export obstacles in the country? What is the influence of preferential trade agreements on the firms' export opportunities?

Main Determinants of Firms' Export Decisions

Understanding why companies begin to export is useful for a better comprehension of firms' export behavior. The main factor in footwear companies' export activity was demand by foreign clients. Some of these were clients from neighboring countries, such as Bolivia or Paraguay. United States–based traders also played an important role in encouraging exports in this industry: they were looking for manufacturers to replace Brazilian suppliers. These traders also contributed to a significant upgrading of the footwear companies by enabling them to learn to export and by forcing firms to progressively upgrade their production capabilities. After this first stage, managers started trying to get new clients abroad by traveling to other countries in the region or by going to trade fairs. In this respect, footwear firms that export have followed the sequence detailed by Donald Keesing and Sanjaya Lall (1992).

By way of contrast, the main determinant that triggered exporting by Chilean printing firms was the intense competition in the domestic printing industry. The largest printing firms responded to that increased competition by buying new equipment that allowed them better quality products. At the same time, the technological changes of the two past decades increased the optimal production scale in the printing industry. Therefore, the purchase of new equipment implies an increase of scale. This, in turn, given the limited size of the domestic market, has driven the largest printing firms to have a growing presence in export markets.

Exporting relatively large shares of their output allows companies to invest in equipment and management changes required for consistently higher quality levels, which in turn makes it easier for firms to continue exporting. Exporting makes it easier for them to negotiate input prices and get larger export orders, thus enabling them to have access to pecuniary economies of scale.[4]

Meanwhile, for other printing companies, particularly those with a smaller share of the domestic market, exporting is the only way to try to maintain their profits, as their share of the domestic market decreases, also due to the competition that characterizes the industry.

Exporting without the need to upgrade was possible for Chilean printing firms because the intense competition in the domestic market had already pushed them to upgrade. (Chile was the first country in the region to be exposed to strong import competition, and therefore, many firms there had to start upgrading earlier than in other countries.) Indeed, demanding clients in the domestic market forced those companies that wanted to preserve their market share to invest in improving product quality.

Another factor that facilitated exporting was that several Chilean companies were major indirect exporters already. Indeed, some printing firms had already become indirect exporters, even before exporting became an important activity, through the products they supplied to exporters. A typical case is that of the packaging used by Chilean food-processing manufacturers that have become successful exporters of such products as tomato paste.

The intense competition in the Chilean printing market turned the strongest printing firms into companies capable of going out to look for export opportunities in the region. They were helped in this by contacts provided by clients in Chile. For example, when the managers of the printing companies decided to try to export regularly, instead of just selling to occasional foreign clients, they contacted their clients in the domestic market and asked them for recommendations to related companies abroad. Once a company was able to start selling to a subsidiary of a transnational corporation in another Latin American country, it became much easier to get other clients in that new market.

Therefore, the factor that set off exports by the Chilean printing industry is different from the one that was determinant for the footwear firms included in the survey: it is a supply-push process, much more than a demand-pull one. In other words, there was not one single main factor behind the export push in these Chilean firms: footwear firms started exporting due to demand from foreign clients; printing firms did so for reasons related to the technology required by a demanding domestic market.

Learning When Exporting

The study of export and nonexport firms showed that export companies have greater learning opportunities than nonexport ones due to contacts with traders and foreign clients and to exposure to international competition. This learning takes place in matters directly related to exporting. Nevertheless, it also takes place in matters not as directly related to selling abroad, such as production guidelines, quality control procedures, product specifications, and management practices. These enhanced learning opportunities allow companies to get on a steeper learning curve, accumulate greater knowledge, and thus have access to dynamic economies of scale. Exporting simultaneously encourages firms to upgrade while, at the same time, providing them with greater opportunities to do so. This allows companies to preserve and increase their market share both at home and abroad.

The first step firm managers must take when they are planning to begin exporting is to gather information. When Chilean footwear entrepreneurs started exporting, they needed to learn how to get clients abroad, set up the logistics required to export, and find out which were the customary financial arrangements. They also needed information about access to the export promotion instruments and relevant trade fairs for their market segment. ProChile and ASEXMA assisted the firms in obtaining information, and, at the same time, traders helped them to start getting their plants organized for export.

Printing firms had an easier time gathering the information needed to begin exporting because selling abroad had become an established practice by the time this industry began to export regularly. Another factor that contributed to the industry's relative ease in beginning to export was that the largest firms already had updated products as a result of intense competition in the domestic market and of upgrading strategies they followed to survive this competition. Moreover, several printing firms were already indirectly exporting significant shares of their output through their sales to Chilean exporters, such as those with wrapping and packaging products.

In addition to getting information on how to break into export markets and fulfill export formalities, for example, Chilean companies also had to learn how to improve the quality of their products and make them appropriate for international markets. Footwear firms benefited from the support provided by traders, participation in trade fairs and the contact with clients, and exposure to international competition. Printing firms benefited mainly from exposure to international competition and from learning how to provide better services to demanding clients.

The greater learning opportunities provided by exporting are, in the long run, one of the strongest advantages export firms have over nonexport companies. The contact with foreign markets encourages company managers to get information on the latest product specifications, production guidelines, and quality control systems required to meet those specifications. Exporting also puts managers in closer touch with the updated inputs used in the industry and allows the managers to find out which are the best suppliers.

Other areas less directly related to the quality of the product—such as administrative and logistics guidelines—also showed evidence of substantial transformations due to exporting. Hence, exporting has resulted not only in significant changes in the way firms manufactured the goods, but also in how the companies were organized.

The learning process set off by exporting was much stronger in the footwear than in the printing firms, since the latter were already using updated practices before beginning to export. Yet, even printing firms managers stated that exporting had provided their companies with significant learning opportunities that had a positive impact on services supplied to clients, quality of product, and management practices.

Nevertheless, as the Chilean economy has progressively become more open to foreign competition as a result of the combination of trade liberalization and exchange rate appreciation, nonexport firms are changing their practices and behaving increasingly like exporting ones. Their managers now frequently go to trade fairs, travel abroad to visit other companies, and hire consultants so as to change product specifications and production and administrative procedures.

Anyhow, exporting provides firms with significant learning opportunities that allow them to upgrade and to gain market share. Export companies have greater learning opportunities than nonexport firms. Moreover, the learning process stimulated by exporting has positive spillovers in the domestic market, allowing companies there to introduce updated products and practices.

Although the challenge faced by firms in the Chilean industries that confront strong import competition has also stimulated learning in nonexport firms, the strongest learning takes place in companies in close contact with markets abroad. Exporting is, without a doubt, one of the best ways to encourage a dynamic learning process because it encourages faster learning for upgrading, while simultaneously providing firms with greater opportunities to find out what they need to do for that purpose.

Export Promotion Policies

Effective export promotion policies play an important role in encouraging a greater number of firms to export. Yet, these policies are rarely evaluated by firm managers, who are well placed to assess the policies from the standpoint of the users. Interviews with company executives showed that Chile's export promotion system is effective in providing support for companies' export efforts: information is readily available and export formalities are transparent, streamlined, and expeditious.

The instrument most often used by the export firms included in the investigation was the Reintegro Simplificado (a few entrepreneurs had also used the scheme for paying lower tariffs on capital goods). Most of the firms have received assistance from ProChile, particularly when taking the first steps to export. For the most part, company executives felt that Chile's export promotion policies and institutions were effective.

Nevertheless, the firm managers were not as optimistic about the effectiveness of export promotion policies in the future. They were concerned that the elimination of the Reintegro Simplificado and of the scheme allowing them to cut tariffs on equipment would make it more difficult for them to export. Moreover, they felt that although ProChile was very supportive, it needed to improve the quality and the diversity of the services supplied to exporters.

Export Obstacles

Firms' exporting success is a function of their own production and marketing capability, of the effectiveness of export promotion instruments, and of the general economic environment that promotes exporting or, on the contrary, discourages companies from selling abroad. A range of factors, from the state of the country's infrastructure to how customs operates, influences companies' decisions to sells goods abroad. When these factors have a negative influence on companies' abilities to export, the aggregate impact is the *costo país,* that is, the additional cost firms bear simply by exporting from a given country.

The first obstacle to exporting named by corporate managers was the appreciation of the exchange rate discussed above. The second main obstacle to exporting faced by firms in Chile is the poor state of the infrastructure, particularly outside the capital, Santiago. For instance, the companies that export manufactured goods to the Mercosur countries by land have problems in winter, since access to the main tunnel that allows trucks to cross the Andes Mountains is often blocked by snow.

Port facilities will also require substantial investment. The facilities at Valparaiso and San Antonio practically collapse during the harvest season, when shipping fresh fruit in a short period is critical. The country has invested in infrastructure over the past years, yet infrastructure upgrading has lagged behind export growth and has produced bottlenecks.

All the same, export firms in Chile face significantly fewer obstacles than the companies in most other Latin American countries. Chilean exporters do have an advantage over their competitors in the region. Nevertheless, the government should give priority to investment in infrastructure if it wants to promote sustained export growth.

Preferential Trade Agreements

Chile has signed a number of PTAs with several Latin American countries and with Canada during the past years. A rigorous assessment of the impact of the PTAs on Chilean companies would require a longer time and more specific studies. Still, it is possible to draw some general preliminary conclusions from the information obtained during the interviews. The interviews provide a good opportunity for a rough estimate of export firms corporate managers' overall view of the PTAs' influence on export opportunities.

Executives of Chilean companies interviewed saw the PTAs as providing their companies with more opportunities than threats, at least in the long run. There will be a direct positive effect as the PTAs provide Chilean firms with greater export opportunities that allow them to offset the small size of the domestic market.

Moreover, Chilean firms stand to gain more from the PTAs than their counterparts in other countries. The marginal benefit from the decrease in tariffs will be greater for Chilean companies that will then face substantially lower tariffs in other Latin American countries and fewer nontariff barriers. By contrast, competing firms in other countries of the region had already faced low tariffs when selling their products in Chile. Chilean companies will gain from the PTAs not only through the increase of the size of the potential markets for their final products, but also from access to cheaper inputs, as has been, for example, the case with Mexican imports.

Companies exporting manufactured goods stand to benefit most from the PTAs with other countries in South America, where their products can compete with domestic manufacturers. This has been confirmed by studies carried out on this topic (Agosín 1993b).

Conclusions

Chile had high export growth rates during the late 1980s and the early 1990s thanks to sound macroeconomic policies and a trade policy that gave emphasis to opening up the economy. The nation was a pioneer in trade liberalization in Latin America and a model for many other medium and small-sized economies in the region. Furthermore, the unilateral trade liberalization had been complemented with numerous PTAs since the early 1990s, allowing Chilean manufacturing firms to offset the effects of the small domestic market.

At the same time, the country had an effective trade promotion organization, innovative export promotion instruments, streamlined export formalities, and fewer export obstacles than the other countries in the region. These components contributed to a coherent and effective export promotion policy.

Yet, the country's export performance has been increasingly based on specialization in exporting a few natural-resource-intensive commodities. Export products are mainly primary goods with very low processing levels, thus precluding the incorporation of technological innovations that have a strong potential for yielding widespread positive externalities on the economy.

Moreover, the importance of copper has decreased steadily since the 1970s, but it still accounts for over 40% of the country's exports and a significant portion of the revenue of the public sector.

Together with that, there is a strong concentration of export markets: almost half of Chile's exports go to only five countries. Furthermore, there is a significant concentration of export activity in a small number of companies, while a significant proportion of other export firms export only intermittently.

These features of Chile's export performance make the country highly vulnerable to the fluctuations in export markets. For example, the country's exports dropped by over 13% during 1998 in the wake of the economic turbulence in Asia that later spread to Latin America.

Nevertheless, the downturn of exports over the past year is not only due to the aftermath of Asia's economic troubles, but is also the result of macroeconomic policies that got off track in the recent years, at least as far as promoting export growth. The strong appreciation of the exchange rate over a long period combined with an increase in domestic costs has cut exports by Chilean firms. This is particularly true for companies exporting goods that do not benefit from an extraordinary comparative advantage, such as copper, wood, and fish. The long-term effect of appreciation is to discourage investment in export projects for a wide range of industries.

At the same time, another determinant that contributed to dampening export growth is that export promotion policies, in spite of their very good record, are past their peak. New activities introduced by ProChile in the recent past have been insufficient to spark a new export drive. More radical, widespread, and swift measures would have been required to have a sizeable impact. In retrospect, export promotion does not appear to have been a top priority in the government's economic agenda. The policies that contributed to Chile's high export growth rate have run out of steam. The sluggish growth of nontraditional exports most recently is a clear indicator of this. New policies are needed for the country to go back to the high export growth rates of the late 1980s and early 1990s.

This need for new policies is compounded by the fact that the country's export promotion instruments will become less effective for encouraging export diversification once the export subsidies are phased out. Their phasing out is necessary to allow Chile to comply with the country's commitments in the Uruguay Round Agreements. An important share of the medium-sized companies exporting goods other than commodities are heavily dependent on the Reintegro Simplificado, as was demonstrated by the study on the behavior of export firms.

In the absence of a firm set of innovative policies that ultimately lead to export growth and diversification, the most reasonable forecast is that even if export growth is resumed once the demand for commodities in the global markets recovers, nontraditional exports will continue to lag in the long run. This situation will be reinforced if the appreciation of the exchange rate continues at its present level, particularly in comparison with the larger markets in Latin America. In other words, if the present policy mix is carried on, the dampening of nontraditional exports will persist.

It may be that nontraditional exports will increase their rate of growth in the short run as manufacturers try to offset the fall of demand in the domestic market. Yet in the long run, as demand recovers, the rate of growth of nontraditional exports will most probably be weak because the prevailing economic policies do not encourage investment in export-oriented projects, with only the exception of those industries that have extraordinary comparative advantage in natural resources.

The authorities that work closely with exporters, such as ProChile and the Ministry of the Economy, and the exporters' trade associations are clearly concerned about these challenges, particularly in light of the requirement to eliminate export subsidies. They have put together a series of instruments and policy proposals in the program, "Plan de Desarrollo de la Competitividad de Chile 1998–2003."

Some of the proposals in this program seek to strengthen ProChile and its support for encouraging firms to have a regular presence in foreign markets. Another array of measures is aimed at increasing the productivity in a wide range of companies in the country so as to widen Chile's export base. This is a step in the right direction, since the best way to encourage sustained export growth is to progressively increase productivity levels across the economy, for companies selling only on the domestic market and for those that export.[5]

These proposals have the additional advantage of not being aimed exclusively at the exporter, allowing them therefore to be compatible with the Uruguay Round Agreements. Policies to upgrade productivity will probably become more important in the coming years in Latin America because such agreements restrict export subsidies for nonagricultural goods while allowing support that is not directed at exporters.[6] From that standpoint, the program is a useful example for other countries seeking to design an export promotion policy compatible with the new multilateral trade rules.

Nonetheless, even if they are put into practice, the measures presented in the "Plan de Desarrollo de la Competitividad de Chile 1998–2003" will not be sufficient to give the country's exports the thrust needed to regain high growth rates for nontraditional exports and an increasingly diversified export mix.

These proposals could be complemented by the following additional measures:

1. Setting up a program that allows companies that export regularly high volumes of output to fulfill highly streamlined import and export formalities, based on the ALTEX Program from Mexico
2. Revising the current formalities required by the drawback system to facilitate its use by a large number of firms, particularly as the Reintegro Simplificado is phased out
3. Providing assistance for small and medium-sized exporters to enable them to gather the paperwork required for using the drawback
4. Improving the instruments used for export financing and insurance
5. Carrying out a complete revision of the current export promotion instruments to establish their effectiveness (any instrument that is used by less than a handful of firms is either operating below its potential or unnecessary)

Still, the main task that must be tackled at present goes beyond building a piecemeal export promotion policy. If Chile wants to get back to high export growth rates that are sustainable even when there is turbulence in global markets, the country needs a new, coherent set of policies aimed at encouraging export growth and diversification. This implies policies designed to promote widespread increases in productivity.[7] The government must also assign a high priority to investments in infrastructure projects with the goal of facilitating exporting. In addition, ProChile needs to be allowed a greater autonomy, an increase of its funding, and a tightening of its links to private-sector organizations, as described in the project sent to Chile's Congress.

At the same time, there is a need for an exchange rate policy that is simultaneously stable in the long run and conducive to investment in a wide variety of export industries: long-term currency appreciation should reflect increases in productivity. It must be stressed that even the best export promotion policies will be powerless for increasing exports if the long-term exchange rate is systematically appreciated. Past experience in Chile itself has demonstrated that exchange rate policies play a key role in export performance (Agosín 1993b).

In the short run, exporters are the ones who bear the cost of the lower export growth rate. In the long run, the cost will be borne by the country as it reinforces its export specialization in a few commodities and the option of exporting goods with higher value added is relinquished. Moreover, given the importance of export growth as a motor for the rest of the economy, the decrease in export growth rates may lead to lower GDP growth rates over the long run.

In sum, to have effective export promotion policies, the issue that the government and the private sector must address at present is the design of a new, coherent, comprehensive, and effective export promotion strategy that allows it to increase export growth rates and diversification. The decision to design and adopt this policy must be a priority for the government and the private sector. The government must provide evidence that it is committed to this goal. In the absence of such a commitment at the highest level, the country will continue to face a dwindling growth in nontraditional exports and will reinforce the specialization in a few export commodities. Therefore, it will be increasingly vulnerable to external shocks.

Notes

1. The information included in this section, unless otherwise specified, is from ECLAC (1999b) and (1999c) and from preliminary data from ECLAC based on official figures.

2. Chile has other policy instruments to support firm upgrading, such as partial subsidies of the cost of hiring consultants for management, environment, and design capability, among other areas. These instruments, which seek to encourage the demand for such activities by firms, are often related to export activities. Nevertheless, they were not included here because they are not specifically oriented toward export firms. For example, companies have access to the Fondos de Asistencia Técnica (FAT), the Proyectos de Fomento (PROFO), and the Fondo Nacional de Desarrollo Tecnológico y Productivo (FONTEC). There are also centers managed by trade associations that seek to promote firm upgrading, such as the Centro de Productividad Industrial (CEPRI). They have played a significant role in improving export supply capability by allowing firms to upgrade.

3. This section is based on Carla Macario (1998b).

4. Input procurement is not always considered a source of economy of scale because the reduction of costs takes place outside the production process and does not imply a shift of the production function. Therefore, this kind of economy of scale is sometimes described as pecuniary economy of scale.

5. See Macario (1998c) for a description of the "Plan de Desarrollo de la Competitividad de Chile 1998–2003."

6. See Wilson Peres (1997) for a thorough presentation of the competitiveness policies in Latin America.

7. See Manuel Agosín and Ricardo Ffrench-Davis (1998) for policy recommendations aimed at upgrading productivity in Chile.

4

Brazil: The Challenge of Improving Export Performance

Regis Bonelli

The expansion in Brazil's international trade links has been reflected in stronger flows of goods and services, as well as in financial flows, since the early 1970s. There has also been a long-term increase in exports based on natural resources and skilled labor products and, to a lesser extent, of exports from the metalworking industry. Nevertheless, it is difficult to tell whether the positive performance of the late 1980s was the result of an aggressive foreign exchange policy, of the growth in the world economy, or of the existence of widespread idle capacity in the Brazilian economy for many years, especially in industry. In recent times this scenario has undergone significant changes, particularly since 1994.[1]

Trade and financial liberalization in Brazil since the early 1990s has gone hand in hand with a successful stabilization process, since mid-1994. One of the least understood, or most controversial, aspects of stabilization is foreign exchange policy. The importance of this policy in the adjustment of domestic and external prices contrasts with the policy's role as a source of competitiveness, in light of the "strong *real*" policy that characterized Brazil's exchange rate up to the beginning of 1999. It has also been observed that the cornerstone of Brazil's stabilization process is the combination of foreign exchange policy and trade liberalization: it is the open economy that keeps price increases for tradables in check and causes prices of nontradables to become stable over the medium and long term. Clearly, this was possible thanks to the existence of a deindexed exchange rate.

Exports play a vital role in this new context of foreign exchange policy and external trade liberalization. The strategy pursued by Brazil requires export growth to avoid balance-of-payments problems, especially since trade liberalization coupled with an exchange rate anchor makes imports extremely attractive, thus potentially jeopardizing the external trade balance. Thus exports need to grow primarily as a source of foreign exchange, rather than as a source of growth for industrial and agricultural output.[2] Policies to promote exports assume a central role in strategies like that chosen by Brazil, since they cannot rely on a boost to exports resulting from the low levels of utilization of installed industrial capacity nor on an undervalued exchange rate, as was the case with the export drive of the 1970s and early 1980s.

The fact that it is not possible to rely on an undervalued exchange rate to boost exports adds an additional cost to economic policy, and requires that policymakers show a great deal of skill. The solution adopted—which has acquired a greater importance over the medium term—is based on the implementation of measures aimed at reducing the so-called Brazil cost, that is, the implicit cost entailed in a range of charges, inefficiencies, and transport and communications costs that reduce the systemic competitiveness of Brazil's production, particularly its exports.

Brazil's export performance over the past years has been lackluster, owing to the above factors. However, it is essential to boost export growth over the medium and long term, lest the current stabilization-cum-growth strategy be jeopardized. What means has the Brazilian government used to pursue this strategy? What has been the experience at the microeconomic level of firms engaged in exporting? What obstacles have there been to expanding exports, especially nontraditional ones? Is there a learning process associated with exporting? Which government measures have proved most effective in stimulating exports, and how do companies rate the existing instruments?

These are a few of the questions that this chapter attempts to answer, using empirical evidence provided by field interviews with twelve firms from four manufacturing industries: car parts, pulp and paper, machinery and equipment, and textiles. The diversity of the industries selected helped enrich the analysis and set policy proposals in a more real-world context.

The Macroeconomic Environment

Main Characteristics of Brazil's Recent Macroeconomic Policies

The 1990s have been a period of significant change for Brazil's economy and society. On the one hand, the economy has been stabilized after nearly 15 years of high inflation, which was also irregular, but showed an upward trend. On the other, the country has experienced trade and financial liberalization on a scale that seemed unthinkable up until only a few years ago. One of the consequences of this transformation has been that the degree of openness of the Brazilian economy—measured by the sum of imports and exports over GDP—has almost doubled, going from 11.1% in 1990 to 20.2% in 1998 (see Table 4.1).[3]

After forty years of accelerated growth, marked by only brief interruptions, the economy went into a period of unprecedented stagnation between 1981 and 1992. Over this period, GDP grew by a mere 16% while population increased by 26%, resulting in a loss of per capita income of roughly 8%. Brazilian industry, in particular, was producing less in 1992 than in 1980! As could be expected, the contraction in output came with deep pessimism and disillusionment. The investment rate in constant 1980 U.S. dollars—a barometer of the corporate sector's expectations—fell from an average of 23.3% of GDP in the 1970s to around 18.3% in the 1980s and to barely 13.6% in 1992.[4]

The recessions of 1981–1983 and 1990–1992 had very little effect, if any, on the inflation rate, since the Brazilian economy functioned with ever more refined and generalized indexation mechanisms. The result was that in 1993, on the eve of implementation of the *Real* Plan, the inflation rate had reached a whopping 2,600% per year.

Between 1986 and 1992, Brazil experienced a total of five stabilization plans, most of which imposed wage and price freezes and voided contractual agreements, without producing any long-lasting effects. Indeed, the main result was to increase uncertainty among economic agents and reduce the credibility of successive governments and economic teams.

By contrast, the economy's performance over 1993–1995 was exceptional. GDP rose by about a cumulative 15%, or 10% in per capita terms. GDP increased another 2.9% in 1996 and 3.8% in 1997. By contrast, growth was interrupted in 1998 as Brazil faced the aftermath of the turbulence in Asia. The growth standstill has significant consequences for the region because Brazil's is by far the largest economy in the region, with an output of over US$700 billion for 1998 (in 1995 prices), that is almost 40% of Latin America's GDP.

In the mid-1990s, investment rates increased, though only moderately, reaching close to 16% (in 1980 prices). The quality of investment improved substantially, with an ever increasing share of capital investment accounted for by machinery and equipment, especially imported, whose technological content is clearly higher. With all that, labor pro-

Table 4.1 Brazil: Economic Indicators

	1990	1991	1992	1993	1994	1995	1996	1997	1998[g]
GDP[a]	571,293	576,828	575,232	601,216	638,662	665,422	684,460	710,223	711,870
GDP growth rates[b]	–4.6	1.0	–0.3	4.5	6.2	4.2	2.9	3.8	0.2
Imports[a,c]	22,603	24,289	25,455	33,930	43,618	63,293	65,902	80,896	81,945
Exports[a,c]	40,641	39,640	45,569	51,432	53,074	52,641	51,734	58,189	61,771
Import ratio[d]	4.0	4.2	4.4	5.6	6.8	9.5	9.6	11.4	11.5
Export ratio (all goods)[d]	7.1	6.9	7.9	8.6	8.3	7.9	7.6	8.2	8.7
Export ratio (manufactures)[e]	51.9	54.8	56.9	58.7	54.8	53.1	53.1	53.1	54.2
Exchange rate[f]	0.000025	0.00015	0.0016	0.032	0.64	0.92	1.01	1.08	1.16

Source: ECLAC (1999b) and (1999c), and other information from ECLAC, on the basis of official figures.
a. Millions of U.S. dollars at 1995 prices.
b. Average annual rates at 1995 prices.
c. Goods and services.
d. Percentages of GDP at 1995 prices. Includes goods and services.
e. Percentages of total value of FOB exports of goods.
f. Nominal exchange rate in *reals* per dollar.
g. Preliminary figures.
Information is from different sources, so there may be discrepancies.

ductivity, measured in terms of gross output (rather than added value), expanded by 34% in 1993–1995. The share of manufacturing was 21.1% in 1997.

Inflation as measured by the general price index dropped considerably, falling to around 10% in 1996 (January–December). Table 4.1 summarizes some of the macroeconomic indicators for the period 1990–1998.

At the same time the role of the state in the economy has been radically transformed. Trade and financial liberalization, declining barriers to entry and exit, a more open approach to the role of foreign capital, and the lifting of price controls are all increasingly part of the economic landscape in Brazil. This is in line with the trend observed in other Latin American countries.

The economy was successfully stabilized thanks to the *Real* Plan, an ambitious program that involved the deindexation of prices, the exchange rate, and wages without any termination of contracts. In fact, the *Real* Plan constitutes a bold change in the thrust of economic policy. The plan was implemented in three stages.[5] The first stage consisted of a temporary adjustment to the public accounts, which produced a lower operating deficit in 1993 than in 1992 and enabled a surplus to be posted in 1994. Next, an Emergency Social Fund was set up, renamed the Fiscal Stabilization Fund upon its extension, which was approved by Brazil's Congress in February 1994. The fund made it possible for the government to freely reallocate (or choose not to spend) 20% of funds in question (previously earmarked for specific areas and ministries).

The second stage of the plan was launched in March 1994 with the creation of the unit of real value (URV), an accounting unit set daily at par with the value of the U.S. dollar. The unit was an ingenious indexation mechanism that made it possible to align prices, wages, and inflationary expectations. Thus, during the four-month transition period in which the URV was in force, relative prices were realigned (though not completely), thus avoiding the residual inflation that would probably mar the third stage of the plan, as happened with other stabilization initiatives both in Brazil and in other Latin American countries. At the same time, there were concerns—which proved unfounded—that the speedup in inflation that would follow the introduction of the URV (on account of the widespread use of daily indexation, with the indexation period dropping from longer periods, as before) would get inflation out of control. The increase in the inflation rate was only moderate by Brazilian standards, though. As a result, prices and wages were not frozen because certain guidelines were established in respect to wages, rents, school tuition, and other activities.

The third stage of the plan began on 1 July 1994, once all prices and wages had been converted into URVs (i.e., units of account). The government proceeded to change all the currency in circulation, along with its name. Henceforth, prices were quoted in *reals*, rather than URVs, thus making the *real* a means of payment and not just a unit of account (as the URV had been).

The drastic slowdown in inflation led to an immediate increase in real incomes and credit, and this reinforced the upswing in economic growth already evident in 1993. Consumer durables in particular benefited from this situation. Output of these goods grew by an impressive 47% between the last quarter of 1992 and the last quarter of 1994. At the same time, "the combination of a monetary policy of high interest rates and a foreign exchange policy consisting of an 'asymmetrical band' caused the *real* to appreciate vis-à-vis the dollar, from a one-to-one parity at the outset of the plan to R$0.846 to the dollar in late December 1994, a nominal appreciation of 15%, which thus contributed to an additional decline in the exchange rate-wage ratio."[6]

By the end of 1994, the rise in domestic demand, which was increasingly met through import growth, led to an increase in the levels of installed capacity utilization—along with the risk of inflationary pressures—and a rapid worsening of the trade balance. This was the backdrop to the Mexican crisis. The outflow of international capital that followed threatened to upset Brazil's stabilization unless tough measures to control aggregate demand, such as interest rate hikes and stiff credit controls, were put in place. Such measures were duly implemented in the first half of 1995. In March 1995, the adoption of a floating band contributed to a real devaluation of the *real*.

The imposition of high short-term interest rates generated substantial net foreign capital inflows, temporarily relieving balance of payments constraint after reserves had declined by about US$10 billion in the first half of 1995. In addition, there was a marked slowdown in the level of economic activity, with quarterly GDP declining in the second and third quarters of that year.

The financial situation of various firms and banks was aggravated by a number of factors: the drop in the level of activity, along with high interest rates; substantial wage rises granted by firms that still harbored doubts about the changes in economic policy; mounting debts contracted during the consumer and investment boom of 1994; and the impact of the intensification of trade liberalization. The volume of loans overdue rose, aggravating the problems of commercial banks that were already facing losses from the end of spreads that had allowed profits during the high inflation period.

The fragility of the financial system was obvious. The government was beset by a serious crisis of confidence until it implemented a plan to restructure private banks. High interest rates claimed another victim, the public accounts, owing to the debts racked up earlier by all three levels of government and the need to issue high interest bonds to reduce the liquidity that would result from the capital flows attracted by high interest rates. Accordingly, the balance of the consolidated public sector as a proportion of GDP shifted from a surplus of 1.34% in 1994 to a deficit of 5.00% in 1995, nearly half of which was accounted for by states and municipalities. Interest rates had a clear role in this deterioration; the expenditure on interest went from 3.8% of GDP in 1994 to 5.4% in 1995.

This shows that the key challenge faced by the adjustment and stabilization of Brazil's economy is how to cut the public deficit. Accordingly, the states and municipalities are making efforts, along with the federal government, to renegotiate debt, though the process has not been without its setbacks. Still, the operational deficit reached about 5.0% of GDP in 1997, while the balance-of-payments deficit on current account reached 4.2% of GDP. This brings us to an examination of trends in the external accounts, and in particular of the role and recent performance of exports, a key variable in the success of Brazil's stabilization strategy.

Export Performance

One of the few disappointing results of Brazil's macroeconomic performance since the implementation of the *Real* Plan has been sluggish export growth. Consequently, Brazil has posted a trade deficit since 1995, something that had not happened since 1980. For a number of analysts, the rapid deterioration of the balance of payments is a cause for concern. However, the authorities do not seem overly perturbed by this trend, since Brazil has a high level of international reserves.

Slow export growth reflects the fact that Brazil's exports have not kept pace with the growth in world trade: Brazil accounted for around 1.4% of world exports in 1979, but this figure had fallen to just 0.897% in 1995, a result often attributed to the revaluation of the local currency. Table 4.2 illustrates the degree of processing in merchandise exports. The table shows that the bulk of Brazil's exports are made up of goods

Table 4.2 Brazil: Profile of Exports: Value FOB and Breakdown, 1989–1996 (Percentage)[a]

Year	Value[b]	Commodities	Semimanufactures	Manufactures
1989	34,405	28.9	16.9	54.2
1990	31,414	29.4	16.3	54.2
1991	31,620	27.6	14.8	56.2
1992	35,862	24.7	14.4	59.7
1993	38,592	24.3	14.1	60.8
1994	43,545	25.4	15.8	57.3
1995	46,506	23.6	19.7	55.0
1996	47,746	25.5	17.5	55.3

Source: FUNCEX (Center for the Studies of Foreign Trade Foundation) bulletins, various issues.

a. Totals do not add up to 100% because special transactions are not included. Some of the main commodities are iron ore, soya meal, raw coffee beans, ground soya, and leaf tobacco. Some of the main semimanufactures are pulp, raw aluminum, soybean oil, granulated sugar, and iron and steel semimanufactures.

b. Millions of U.S. dollars.

featuring some degree of processing. At least three-quarters of exports are processed products, even though a substantial proportion involves only a small amount of processing and value added.

R. Iglesias (1996) shows that the difficulties experienced by Brazilian exports are not only attributable to the "strong *real*" policy. Exports began to loose momentum long before that, since the late 1970s.[7] For example, between 1974 and 1979, Brazil's total exports grew at an average rate of 14.1% per year, but this figure fell to 10.2% in 1980–1985 and again to 8.8% in 1986–1989. Table 4.2 indicates that exports grew at barely 5.1% on average over 1989–1995. For 1996 the rate fell to 2.7%. This loss of dynamism was due in part to domestic factors, since both the world economy and the trends in prices of nonoil commodities were favorable to Brazil's exports during most of the period in question (except for 1996).

Furthermore, it can be demonstrated that the real effective exchange rate was high (indicating loss of competitiveness) in a number of periods when Brazil's export returns were mediocre, such as in 1986, the year of the *Cruzado* Plan. In particular, export returns were especially poor in the wake of the (largely unsuccessful) stabilization plans, irrespective of the real exchange rate. It appears that growth in domestic demand, and not just the exchange rate, explains export results (in addition to export prices, growth in trade and the level of activity in the world economy). Table 4.3 summarizes the relevant information.

Table 4.3 Brazil: Export Growth—The Real Effective Exchange Rate and Level of Activity

Year	Export growth (%)	Real effective exchange rate (1990=100)	GDP growth (%)	Growth in manufacturing output (%)
1985	–5.06	160.0	7.8	2.0
1986	–12.83	166.7	7.5	2.7
1987	17.34	159.1	3.6	–9.3
1988	28.85	156.6	–0.05	–3.4
1989	1.76	1100	3.2	2.9
1990	–8.64	100.0	–4.4	9.5
1991	0.66	117.3	0.4	–2.4
1992	13.41	124.5	–0.8	–4.1
1993	7.63	119.0	4.2	8.0
1994	12.82	108.3	5.9	7.9
1995	6.80	99.6	4.2	1.7

Source: Iglesias (1996).

Thus, export performance appears to be associated with the slowdown in domestic demand—which enables utilization of idle capacity with a view to redirecting sales toward the external market—and to the relative prices (i.e., real exchange rate changes). In addition, export results also vary according to the progress in regional integration initiatives and to the exchange rate for the Argentine peso (Argentina was the most dynamic market for Brazilian exports in 1991–1994).[8] A further factor contributing to the unsatisfactory export performance, since the late 1980s, was the insufficient expansion of production capacity oriented toward exports.

In light of the option of adopting the exchange rate anchor, albeit with devaluations in line with a periodically readjusted band, the description presented above suggests that future prospects for export growth should not rest on a devalued exchange rate. The alternative economic policy pursued has pinned many of its hopes for improved export performance and trade balance on enhancing systemic competitiveness through lowering the "Brazil cost," and specific trade policies. This will be discussed below.

Trade and Industrial Policies

June 1990 marked the adoption of the most important package of industrial policy and external trade measures seen in Brazil: the General

Guidelines on Industrial Policy and Foreign Trade (PICE), which announced a new tariff structure to be gradually implemented over the following five years (1990–1994). In 1994, the modal import tariff would be 20%, with a ceiling of 40% and an average rate of 14%. Given the natural protection provided by transport, insurance, and port costs in the 20–40% range—depending, for example, on how far away the supplier was located—the arrangements offered a satisfactory level of protection under normal economic conditions and in light of the timetable for the implementation of tariff reduction.[9] Table 4.4 details the changes made to the tariff structure since the program was launched.

The changes introduced to the tariff reduction schedule in late 1994, toward the end of the administration of Itamar Franco, represented the final phase of the trade liberalization process.[10] In early 1996, an average import tariff of 12% came into force, and no significant import restrictions remained.

As already discussed, one of the features of the stabilization program introduced on 1 July 1994, the *Real* Plan, was cutting the link between the exchange rate and domestic price movements—that is, the deindexation of the exchange rate. A combination of the residual inflation during the first months of the plan, huge foreign capital inflows, and use of the exchange rate as an anchor for the prices of tradables contributed to breaking the link between the exchange rate and general price index changes.

Any discussion of the direction of competitiveness policies in Brazil should begin by acknowledging that economic policy making has given top priority to the goal of stabilization. With regard to industrial and foreign trade policies, the government has justified a number of exceptional protectionist measures recently taken by pointing to the need to stabilize the trade balance or shore up employment in industries

Table 4.4 Brazil: Tariffs, 1990–1995 (Percentage)

Date	Average	Mode	Mean	Range	Standard Deviation
1990	32.2	40	30	0–105	19.6
February 1991	25.3	20	25	0–85	17.4
January 1992	21.2	20	20	0–65	14.2
October 1992	16.5	20	20	0–55	10.7
July 1993	14.9	20	20	0–40	8.2
January 1995	12.1	14	10	0–20	6.1

Source: A. C. Pinheiro (1996).

hardest hit by trade liberalization. In addition, any trade liberalization program has a long-term goal of reducing protection by seeking to bring the range of domestic relative prices in line with international ones, thus shifting the allocation of resources over the long term toward those tradables that can be produced most efficiently.

Competition from imported products, in a context of a *relatively* high exchange rate had a clearly beneficial impact on price stability in the post–*Real* Plan period owing to the competition's effect on demand. However, supply factors assume greater importance over the longer term. The liberalization of trade entails changes to the productive structure that streamline resource use and improve the quality of final products. The overall result is to lower the costs of production, with predictable effects on price stability. Imports of raw materials and capital goods have benefited from substantially lower interest rates on foreign loans compared with domestic ones. That has helped improve the competitivity of domestic goods, partially offsetting the high interest rates hitherto prevailing in the domestic market (especially for working capital), even though rates showed declines from late 1995 onward.

Export Promotion Policies

The specific export promotion measures adopted by Brazil during the 1990s were of a financial nature, which explains why they attracted considerable attention. A brief presentation of the main mechanisms is presented below.[11] That is followed by a discussion of the measures taken to reduce the "Brazil cost." It should be pointed out that it is the financial type of export promotion measures and schemes to reduce the "Brazil cost" that have undergone the most rapid and exhaustive changes recently.

Export Financing[12]

Export financing is becoming a well-established mechanism in Brazil. The private sector has been involved in financing exports of goods with short production runs through advances on currency exchange contracts (or ACCs, the acronym in Portuguese), advances on export contracts (or ACEs, the acronym in Portuguese), and securitization of exports. With respect to goods with longer production runs, such as machinery and equipment and engineering services, financing is provided by the government through such agencies as the National Bank for Economic and

Social Development (BNDES) and such programs as PROEX Programa de Financiamiento de Exportações, administered by the Banco do Brasil. A brief description of some of the main export financing instruments in Brazil today is given below.[13]

In the case of the BNDES, the most traditional financial product is the Fundo de Financiamento de Exportações (FINAMEX) program, comprising indirect operations (i.e., through agents) aimed at financing exports of machinery and equipment, both for preshipment (since late 1990) and postshipment (since 1991). An examination of the performance of the FINAMEX program between 1993 and 1995 allows us to conclude that the results achieved are meager, given the volume of Brazil's exports of machinery and equipment. In fact, out of total merchandise exports that qualify for financing by the program, estimated at US$6.29 billion in 1995, the amount actually financed came to only US$373 million.

In the second semester of 1995, FINAMEX set up a new instrument, the Fundo de Amparo ao Trabalhador-Cambial (FAT-Cambial) aimed at Brazilian producers competing internationally. It also allowed the program, Financiamento às Empresas (FINEM) (the traditional BNDES financing facility for companies) to be used for export-oriented investments. Success has been very limited in both cases, with FINEM being confused, for practical purposes, with financing for working capital. In fact, the Manufacturing Exports Promotion Program, which was forecast to cover up to US$1 billion, found no takers. This was because industries that were interested in this instrument felt that the financial conditions imposed for assistance to the ten selected manufacturing sectors (namely, 5% and 6.5% over Libor, depending on the sector) were unfavorable.

Those results prompted the government, acting through the BNDES, to seek alternative instruments for financing exports. A set of measures introduced in October/November 1996 broadened the scope of BNDES by including exports of capital goods, engineering services, and turnkey plants as eligible for financing on request.

Another export-financing program is PROEX, which is operated by the Banco do Brasil. The aim of PROEX, created in June 1991, is twofold: financing of exports of goods and services and equalization of interest rates.[14] Export financing was not regulated until the end of 1995. The Central Bank and the Ministry of Industry, Commerce, and Tourism (MICT) have issued regulations that stipulate financing terms and the list of goods and services eligible for assistance. In practice, the Banco do Brasil directs requests for financing to the Export Credit

Committee, a body made up of several government agencies that determines whether to extend credit through the PROEX program. The terms provide for interest rates equivalent to the Libor rate fixed in respect to the period of financing or variable in accordance with the payback period, with maturities ranging from 18 to 120 months, depending on the merchandise financed. Financing covers 85% of the value of merchandise with a minimum local content of 60%, and the proportion financed declines relative to the decrease in local content.

The interest rate equalization mechanism was also regulated by the Central Bank and MICT toward the end of 1995, with rules that set out new criteria for the eligibility of goods and services. Equalization operations totaled US$243.3 million in 1995, with US$194.2 million approved and US$49.1 million paid out. Financing operations amounted to US$80.9 million, with US$32.6 million approved and US$48.3 million paid out. Clearly, these figures are barely a fraction of the volume of export transactions.

Financing for prepayment of exports was regulated in June 1991 by the Central Bank. Merchandise exports qualify for early payment using resources obtained from importers and other forms of financing, over a period of up to 180 days between the date of the exchange contract and the date the goods are actually shipped. Interest rates on the transaction are freely agreed to between the contracting parties, without any Central Bank interference. Such a hands-off approach to interest rates tends to promote competition. That tends to increase the amount of external liquidity available for financing Brazilian exports.

Banks dealing in foreign currency grant advances on ACCs. This instrument entails either the partial or the total early payment of the local currency equivalent of the amount of foreign currency purchased in advance from those exporters by the bank. It is the advance of the cost in foreign currency that the bank negotiating the foreign exchange grants the exporter. The aim is to provide the exporter with funds to undertake the different activities associated with production and selling, thus acting as an export incentive. The advance is obtained at below market cost.[15]

Advances on ACCs can be granted at two stages. In the first stage, the advance is granted anywhere up to 180 days before shipment (financing of production). The second type of advance is granted with the merchandise already shipped, and may be requested up to 60 days after shipment. If entered into at this stage, the contract is known as an ACE, and the term may be extended up to 180 days from the date of shipment.

The maximum term for advances on ACCs varies depending on the Central Bank's interest in administering inflows of foreign exchange, and may extend to 180 or even 360 days. The drawer of an advance on an ACC that does not have the merchandise at time of shipment is required to pay a financial transaction tax (IOF) for breach of contract. Regulations have recently been modified.

One gauge of the importance of this mechanism (ACC) is that of the total flow of foreign currency used to finance exports in 1994, about 87.6% were in the form of the advances and early payment.[16] In 1995 the proportion of funds accounted for by advances, and early payment reached 89.1% and in the first half of 1996, 87.4%.

Another mechanism to provide exporting with financial support is the export note, a contract by which export credit is extended. Under this type of contract, the exporter obtains funds in the country together with local investors, banks, or businesses. After signing a contract, the exporter transfers sale rights to the investor in return for a cash amount in Brazilian *reals* equivalent to the value in foreign currency. Thus the funds are used to finance the production run.

In the meantime, securitization of exports is becoming increasingly widespread in Brazil, especially for large export contracts. This instrument, established by the Central Bank in July 1991, entails the issuance of a security in the international market based on future export sales. It is useful because external financing costs are lower than domestic ones. Another option is loan securitization, which provides, since late 1996, a legal means for exporters to obtain abroad up to 200% of the value of exchange contracts they had held up until 31 July 1996, with no need to pay the IOF. One of the results of the new measure has been a drop in the volume of new advances, currently replaced by the method of raising funds promoted in the resolution described above.[17]

Export Credit Insurance

In October 1996 the credit insurance mechanism was finally regulated.[18] The purpose of this mechanism is to provide insurance against political, extraordinary, and commercial risks. The federal government, through the Brazilian Reinsurance Institute, a state-owned agency, covers political risks. The federal government's share of any net losses is limited to a maximum of 85%, with the balance borne by the insured party. The total limit of insurance coverage is approximately US$3 billion. A term of up to five years is contemplated, but this may be extended to twelve years to cover exports of capital goods with lengthy production periods, as well as exports of engineering services.

An incorporated insurance company whose equity is mostly privately held undertakes coverage of commercial risks: the Sociedade de Crédito à Exportação. The company is owned by the Banco do Brasil, with up to a 30% stake, and the French agency Compagnie Française d'Assurance pour le Commerce Extérieur. Other traditional Brazilian insurers, Sul América and Bradesco, are also candidates to take equity stakes.

Other Financial and Fiscal Mechanisms

One important measure taken recently was the decision to exempt exports of semimanufactured goods and commodities from the merchandise and services sales tax (ICMS), that is, a value-added tax. The measure was to start in August 1996, and the exemption, which had previously applied to manufacturing exports, is now extended to other products, including purchases of investment goods on the domestic market and electricity used in production (both from November 1996 onward). Beginning in 1998, the measure has also been extended to consumer goods used in production. In essence, all these measures are designed to reduce the "Brazil cost."

The credit squeeze caused by the still rather high interest rates prevailing in mid-1996—despite the new BNDES lines (FAT-Cambial)—prompted the monetary authorities to search for alternatives to prevent the trade balance from registering a substantial deficit and to sustain the level of economic activity, especially in manufacturing. Accordingly, in early September 1996, the Central Bank proceeded to create a new form of financing in a bid to enhance export competitiveness and reduce the difficulties for obtaining credit faced by export firms that had concluded contracts with foreign parties, but had yet to ship the merchandise. Resources for the financing facility are to be raised abroad through the banking system and made available to exporters, and have some advantages over preexisting options. In addition, loans granted through this facility are exempt from the IOF, which is applied to foreign currency loans with maturities of under five years. The cost of the facility was estimated by the Central Bank at between 11% and 12% per annum. Each exporter will be able to take out a loan equivalent to 200% of the volume of unsettled ACCs, with merchandise yet to be shipped. This indicates how concerned the Central Bank is about assisting firms facing difficulties in producing or shipping goods as arranged.

In regard to measures that are more general and to institutional changes, there have been a number of other initiatives (in general, horizontal policies). The measures aimed at reducing the Brazil cost and changes to the institutional framework, especially in the sphere of trade policy, are particularly important.

Measures to Reduce the Brazil Cost

Measures in this area hold out the most hope of enhancing the competitiveness of Brazil's industry through reductions in various sorts of costs and increased efficiency of infrastructure. The measures are also the slowest to implement and to yield results. They encompass a broad range of processes from tax breaks for exports to export financing (processes already under way, as discussed above). Other measures include reductions in nonwage labor costs that affect the cost of industrial labor;[19] privatization of concessions for utilities (with the electricity distribution enterprises EXCELSA and Light, and Rede Ferroviária federal Sociedade Anônima, already privatized) and ports; lower interest rates on long-term loans by BNDES (reviewed earlier); enactment of a new law on transport and communications infrastructure; and a project to reduce corporate income tax. In fact, in addition to the negotiations aimed at consolidating the Motor Vehicle Agreement[20] and those on export financing, the main measures taken by the current government have sought to reduce the Brazil cost.[21] The issue of how to increase the "systemic competitiveness" of Brazil's economy will need to be tackled in this manner over the medium and long term. In the short term, efforts are focused on measures to finance exports.

Enhancing Brazil's export competitiveness can be achieved primarily through a combination of the following measures: a reduction in the fiscal cost of exports; improved conditions for financing production of exports and for export financing (including export credit insurance); and greater efficiency and lower costs in port, communications, and transport infrastructure.

As part of the efforts to reduce the fiscal cost of exporting, the payment of social security contributions by the Programa de Integração Social and Contribução para o Financiamento da Seguridade Social levied on purchases in the domestic market of raw materials, intermediate goods, and packaging materials for use in the distribution process was abolished, in the form of a presumptive Industrial Products Tax credit.

With respect to transport and port services infrastructure, expectations are centered on the Utility Concessions Law that authorizes the private sector to lease or operate, among others, toll roads, railways, ports, electricity generation, and distribution companies.

The privatization of Brazil's ports has proceeded at a slow pace, a fact that adversely affects export competitiveness. In a bid to end this situation, the dockyards were included in the National Development Program in early September 1996. Consequently, any decisions concerning privatization of the port system must now be taken at the ministerial level. The dockyards of Río de Janeiro, Bahía, Ceará, São Paulo, Pará, Maranhao, Río Grande do Norte, and Espírito Santo were all affected.

Privatization activity is also anticipated in the telecommunications field. A law has been passed authorizing private interests to operate B-band cellular telephone services, and it is expected that private firms will be invited to bid for satellite exploration. The issue of regulating basic services has come in for rigorous examination, with a view to preventing collusion and other noncompetitive practices.

The tax structure remains under scrutiny, owing to a combination of rapidly increasing exemptions, taxation differentials between groups (which generates inequality), the complexity of the tax system, delays in payment of indemnities/rebates for exporters on some taxes, and, above all, the high tax rates compared with those of other countries. These factors amount to both an explicit and implicit tax on Brazilian exports.

Firms' Export Behavior

The Performance of the Manufacturing Sector

As was the case in other Latin American countries, the development of Brazil's industry was upset by the debt crisis of the early 1980s. The late 1970s had been marked by efforts to adjust the macroeconomic and trade policies, against a backdrop of serious imbalances in the global economy. Nevertheless, the economic team that assumed power in mid-1979 reversed this situation when the team turned to an expansionary economic policy.

The government decided to slow down the level of economic activity at the end of 1980, mainly to curb the trade deficit and generate net export surpluses. The recession that hit Brazil's industry in 1981–1983 highlighted the need to adjust economic policy to cope with the external debt crisis, whose effects would influence the macroeconomic performance for the rest of the decade.

The external debt issue and its repercussions dominated economic policy discussion throughout the 1980s. Therefore, the strategies aimed at promoting industry went against the tide of other developments, such as the speedup in inflation and the recession of 1981–1983, the stagnation that took place after 1986, and, above all, the genuine threat of hyperinflation that loomed toward the end of the 1980s.

It is against this background that the lack of attention paid to manufacturing in that period needs to be examined. Concern about industrial performance had had a low priority, and so in the early 1990s the industrial sector was the same size as ten years earlier. Furthermore, industry no longer generated employment for an ever increasing working population; it operated with substantial idle capacity; and it was more dependent than ever on external demand for growth. Never before had this sector's performance been so mediocre.

At the very beginning of the 1990s, Brazilian industry was hit by a crisis that lasted for three consecutive years (1990–1992). The defensive strategy adopted by many firms, with a drastic reduction in structures and the use of new management techniques, paved the way for a new entrepreneurial mentality and new ways of doing business. Industry did not play a passive role in the face of the new macroeconomic trends, but instead participated actively in a broader restructuring effort, the effects of which have yet to be fully understood.

Beginning in late 1992, however, the liberalization of the economy ushered in a new phase of growth in production. As a result, there followed a period of intense change in firms' internal production structures, while the intersectoral profile remained largely unchanged. In fact, that trend had begun prior to implementation of the *Real* Plan, since the economy, and particularly industry, was emerging from the recession of the early 1990s and showed clear signs of a recovery in installed capacity—though with no corresponding surge in new investments.

Industrial investments in the first half of the 1990s were clearly marginal and defensive in nature, aimed almost exclusively at replacing obsolete equipment and incorporating innovations, without major increases to installed production capacity already in place. The growth in imports of machinery and equipment, parts, and accessories in that period was extraordinary, with domestic products largely replaced by imports. One case in point is the trend in imports of machinery and accessories for the metal products industry, which shot up from US$1.55 billion in 1987–1988 to US$5 billion in 1994–1995. The main feature of industrial performance in the first half of the 1990s, then, was the boom in imports that followed the opening up of foreign trade. This had a substantial impact on manufacturing performance, including some of the sectors studied in this chapter. Furthermore, all the indicators of competitive performance based on export-import ratios showed a considerable worsening.

From the standpoint of trends in production, growth in the 1993–1995 period was led by consumer durable goods-manufacturing sectors. Nondurables also recorded good results, mainly after the stabilization plan, thanks to the reduction of the losses in real income caused by inflation. In fact, the poorest sectors, which make up the bulk of the population, enjoyed huge increases in purchasing power. Not surprisingly, household consumption reached record levels as a result. This was especially so in the initial phase of stabilization. In early 1995, as indicated above, the government was forced to adopt a series of monetary and credit restrictions whose effects were felt in late 1995 and the first half of 1996.

Export performance by industry. Despite huge changes at the microeconomic level in the wake of stabilization, the sectoral profile of Brazil's exports showed relatively little change. Apart from exports whose external prices varied markedly (such as wood pulp), the export profile changed little in the 1990s, although an analysis of the

Table 4.5 Brazil: Yearly Variations in GDP, Investments in Industrial Production, by Selected Periods (Percentage per year)

	1990–1992	1993–1995
Gross domestic product	–1.63	4.76
Fixed capital formation	–7.20	11.02
Capital goods industry	–8.06	9.25
Intermediate goods industry	–4.52	4.03
Consumer durables industry	–4.99	19.37
Consumer nondurables industry	–2.46	4.23
Construction	–7.88	3.61

Source: Brazilian Geographical and Statistical Institute (IBGE).

1985–1995 period as a whole reveals considerable diversification. Tables 4.5 and 4.6 provide the empirical evidence for this.

Evaluation of the Brazilian industrial classification at the two-digit level shows a marked concentration of exports in the manufacturing industry.[22] Exports of primary (i.e., agricultural) products have varied considerably, averaging under 5% of total exports. Mining exports have followed an upward trend, growing at average annual rates of 5–6% between 1985–1987 and 1993–1995, and account for close to 6.5% of total exports.

Processed food products are the main export industry. Up until recently this sector showed signs of losing ground: its relative share of the total declined from almost 28% in 1985 to roughly 20% in 1989–1990, and again to 18% in 1991–1993. However, from then onwards the sector increased its share, reaching 23% in 1995. The evidence suggests that diversification increases when there is export growth and that, on

Table 4.6 Brazil: Exports 1985–1989 (FOB, in Millions of U.S. Dollars)

Categories	1985	1986	1987	1988	1989
Agriculture	1,374	757	1,111	1,195	1,632
Extractive minerals	1,895	1,835	1,846	2,257	2,631
Nonmetallic minerals	159	181	203	267	286
Metallurgical products	2,904	2,801	3,096	5,910	6,303
Metal manufacturing and machinery	844	716	955	1,130	1,477
Electrical and communications equipment	926	1,162	1,247	1,492	1,587
Transport equipment	2,393	2,128	3,401	3,829	3,885
Wood products	299	308	399	504	408
Furniture	43	46	40	45	48
Pulp and paper	562	693	785	1,338	1,307
Rubber	231	199	237	293	282
Chemicals	3,122	1,902	2,338	2,994	2,882
Pharmaceuticals	64	65	88	91	63
Perfumes, soaps, candles	24	25	29	33	43
Plastic products	150	178	95	98	54
Textiles	858	753	1,037	1,090	1,119
Clothing and footwear	1,029	1,080	1,240	1,369	1,411
Hides and skins	210	187	265	446	327
Food products	7,622	6,532	6,936	8,212	7,253
Beverages	9	18	18	24	37
Tobacco products	459	413	432	553	539
Other	210	232	274	323	518
Scrap iron	6	7	6	8	7
Total	27,378	24,202	28,065	35,490	36,090

Source: Department of Foreign Trade (SECEX), Ministry of Industry and Commerce.

the contrary, when the pace of growth declines there is a trend toward export concentration.

The second most important sector is the metallurgical industry, which exhibited significant growth, especially up until 1989. Metallurgical exports increased their share of the total from 11.1% in 1985–1986 to 17.5% in 1989, while the value of all exports combined rose by 32.0% over that same period. In the last two-year period presented in Table 4.6, metal and metallurgical exports reached around US$7 billion, or 14.8% of Brazil's total exports in 1994–1995.

The third most important industry in terms of the value of exports is transport equipment; this sector increased its share of exports from around 9% of the total in 1985–1986 to around 10% in 1994–1995 (i.e., average growth was close to that registered for total exports). In descending order came the following industries, with relative shares in 1985–1986 and 1994–1995 as indicated:

- Chemicals, 9.7% and 7.1%
- Metal manufacturing and machinery, 3% and 5%
- Pulp and paper, 2.4% and 4.9%
- Electrical and communications equipment, 4.1% and 4.4%
- Clothing, footwear, and knitted articles, 4.1% and 3.7%
- Textiles, 3.1% and 2.5%
- Tobacco products, 3.1% and 2.3%
- Wood products, 1.2% and 2.3%
- Rubber products, 0.8% and 1.2%
- Hides and skins, 0.8% and 1.2%

Based on the tables above it is possible to conclude that the industries whose exports increased the most, over the period in question, in decreasing order of average growth rates, were: pulp and paper, wood products, metal manufacturing and machinery, rubber and hides, tobacco products, metallurgical products, transport equipment, and electrical and communications equipment. Roughly speaking, the higher the technological content, the slower the growth of exports.

In respect to the sectors selected for the present study, substantial increases were recorded in industrial machinery, car parts, and paper—though this was not the case for natural, synthetic, or artificial textiles. The inclusion of textiles is because the quality of exported fabrics has changed dramatically and because the industry has undergone an intense transformation.

Table 4.7 Brazil: Exports 1990–1995 (FOB, in Millions of U.S. Dollars)

Categories	1990	1991	1992	1993	1994	1995
Agriculture	1,387	906	1,322	1,487	1,883	1,336
Extractive minerals	2,860	3,079	2,746	2,748	2,779	3,122
Nonmetallic minerals	241	258	321	431	438	481
Metallurgical products	5,389	6,053	6,253	6,350	6,535	7,197
Metal manufacturing and machinery	1,155	1,224	1,510	1,851	2,247	2,370
Electrical and communications equipment	1,444	1,534	1,727	1,917	1,934	2,141
Transport equipment	3,265	3,120	4,265	4,361	4,827	4,366
Wood products	426	443	554	833	1,044	1,082
Furniture	40	58	126	241	267	316
Pulp and paper	1,233	1,264	1,478	1,561	1,825	2,731
Rubber	284	337	443	505	550	578
Chemicals	2,591	2,350	2,594	2,900	3,237	3,363
Pharmaceuticals	69	90	99	105	123	157
Perfumes, soaps, candles	37	49	73	118	120	134
Plastic products	37	45	90	116	120	110
Textiles	1,016	1,142	1,217	1,115	1,133	1,197
Clothing and footwear	1,315	1,371	1,624	2,123	1,825	1,657
Hides and skins	301	319	408	421	481	593
Food products	6,732	6,158	6,861	7,406	9,734	10,821
Beverages	54	67	75	95	150	147
Tobacco products	594	799	960	880	1,010	1,145
Other	558	621	758	775	820	826
Scrap iron	5	15	3	6	21	7
Total	33,025	33,292	37,497	40,337	45,096	47,871

Source: Department of Foreign Trade (SECEX), Ministry of Industry and Commerce.

The Behavior of Export Manufacturing Firms

The interviews were all conducted in the Rio de Janeiro and Sao Paulo areas between October and December of 1996. The results for each industry are presented separately below. A summary of these results is included in the following section.

The first conclusion of interest to this study is that economic liberalization affected the industries under examination in different ways. The effects were felt more strongly in the car parts and the machinery and equipment industries, and less so in the pulp and paper as well as the natural textiles ones.[23]

The car parts industry. The automobile parts industry is of particular interest because it illustrates all the effects of trade liberalization: the effects of a change in the organization and technology of production,

Table 4.8 Brazil: Exports and Imports by Selected Sectors (In Millions of U.S. Dollars)[a]

Year	Machinery for industry	Car parts	Paper and paperboard	Natural textiles
1985	187 (150)	1,121 (379)	251 (71)	155 (2)
1986	123 (280)	997 (565)	332 (129)	151 (4)
1987	146 (445)	1,219 (617)	357 (167)	168 (7)
1988	195 (559)	1,586 (580)	664 (144)	179 (7)
1989	660 (919)	1,571 (599)	598 (257)	177 (17)
1990	516 (1,352)	1,589 (714)	603 (252)	148 (38)
1991	536 (1,382)	1,599 (731)	648 (315)	176 (30)
1992	615 (1,399)	1,849 (942)	699 (219)	237 (19)
1993	865 (1,550)	2,112 (1,322)	783 (280)	226 (44)
1994	1,101 (2,319)	2,334 (1,813)	928 (280)	222 (70)
1995	1,092 (6,081)[b]	2,507 (2,235)	1,215 (821)	241 (866)[c]

Source: Department of Foreign Trade (SECEX), Ministry of Industry and Commerce.
a. FOB for exports and CIF for imports; imports CIF given in brackets.
b. Includes nonindustrial machinery and parts and accessories in 1995.
c. Includes yarn in 1995, imports of which rose from an annual average of just over US$200 million in 1989–1992 to US$799 million in 1993 and US$704 million in 1994.

which has brought about an authentic business revolution in a short period; the impact of global outsourcing; and the effects of the operation of a motor vehicle regime that entitles assembly firms in Brazil to import parts and spare parts at a tariff rate of just 2%, in contrast to 70% for imports of motor vehicles (in the case of makes without a local assembler) or 35% (in the case of makes with a local assembler).

The final outcome has been devastating for the performance of local car parts firms. Nevertheless, the future growth prospects of the motor vehicle industry in Brazil are bright, in light of the potential of Mercosur. This has led to a series of mergers and acquisitions of parts manufacturers in the last couple of years—and it is not coincidental that this has been accompanied by economic stabilization and improved prospects for foreign capital. In fact, throughout 1996 two of the three firms selected were acquired by foreign-owned companies operating internationally in the parts business.

All the firms included in the investigation manufacture car parts, while the Companhia Fabricadora de Peças (COFAP) is also Brazil's leading (and traditional) manufacturer of shock absorbers. Exports had expanded until 1995, when exchange rate movements caused a downturn in the industry. The industry comprises large firms,[24] operating a number of plants, some of which are located abroad.[25]

In regard to technical aspects the degree of vertical integration is generally high, particularly where production is concerned. Purchases of raw materials are concentrated in sheet steel (for COFAP's shock absorbers), powder for the plastic production process (Metal Leve), basic raw materials for bronze parts (Metal Leve), and a number of components (aluminum, silicon). SABO even has a machine-tooling factory. Imports of raw materials (e.g., chemicals) are extremely low, in most cases amounting to less than 5% of total purchases.

However, in all the cases studied outsourcing has made substantial inroads, especially since 1990, in terms of such support services as data processing, cleaning, maintenance, and catering. The trend was evident in all of the manufacturing sectors studied, and accounts in part for the huge productivity gains achieved by Brazilian industry since 1990. This is a more or less obvious aspect of the increased flexibility of manufacturing that has affected practically all industries in Brazil.

As could be expected, because the firms in question are big players and major exporters in their respective business segments, export sales are substantial—especially in contrast to the other sectors analyzed here. Export sales are in the vicinity of US$80 million for Metal Leve, US$130 million for COFAP, and US$25 million for SABO. In the case of some lines, nearly half of production capacity is exported.[26] It is possible to conclude that this is one industry in which exporting provides a spur to business activity, in contrast to some of the other ones examined here. In point of fact, it is hard to envisage these firms surviving in their current form were it not for the exporting link.

It is interesting to note that in all cases, exports are priced slightly below goods sold domestically. This has been especially evident in recent years due to the appreciation of the exchange rate since mid-1994.

All these firms were established or consolidated in the first half of the 1950s, before the car industry was implanted as a result of the Plano de Metas launched by the government of Juscelino Kubitschek (1956–1961). Firms moved into the automobile parts business in the wake of the crisis caused by the shortage of foreign exchange that marked the Brazilian economy throughout the 1950s and that primarily curbed imports of consumer durables, as well as their parts and accessories.[27] Initially devoted to the production of a single item, diversification proceeded apace in the first half of the 1970s to encompass motor vehicle assembly, which was stepped up in the 1970s.

The cycle of export-oriented investment followed a characteristic pattern,[28] and from the mid-1970s onward exports gained momentum thanks to an aggressive policy of support for exports of manufactured goods. Recently, companies have invested in a number of finished plants abroad: COFAP has factories that produce shock absorbers in Portugal and the United States, and SABO is involved with General Motors in a project to manufacture in Detroit.

The interesting conclusion to be drawn is that whether conducted directly or through joint ventures, diversification of investments in the car parts sector has encouraged the creation of manufacturing plants abroad. This poses something of a dilemma for industrial policy. Should the Brazilian government, acting through its agencies, provide assistance, financial or otherwise, to Brazilian firms setting up investments abroad? Thanks to the technologies and methods connected with global outsourcing, this phenomenon is more typically associated with car parts but does not, however, make it any less interesting.

It is noteworthy that imported equipment is playing an increasingly important role in the investment cycle, except in the case of SABO, which manufactures a good part of its own equipment. The lead time varies from one to two years, depending on the type of product manufactured. In all cases, it is possible to make net marginal investments (i.e., those that increase output without the need to invest *en bloc* to create a production unit). In other words, modular investment is possible even in areas such as smelting, and working three shifts is not uncommon, depending on the level of demand.

As regards marketing, firms in the sector sell directly to customers because two of them have foreign subsidiaries. This situation is reinforced by the fact that a substantial portion of exports has a captive market composed of customers (car assembly firms) that make regular purchases of original equipment.[29] None of these firms goes through trading companies or dealers. Some firms have their own offices abroad, along with sales and engineering departments. All firms have underlined the importance of participating in trade fairs at home and abroad (especially the fair held in Frankfurt, Germany).

Firms began exporting for different reasons, in decreasing order of importance: technology development (updating technology); diversification; and boosting overall sales (using BEFIEX, a now defunct export promotion program). Competing abroad encompasses a number of factors: technology and quality; price (especially in foreign markets); and availability of the logistics of product delivery and complementary services.

The exporting strategy of two of the firms analyzed depends on the level of domestic demand, and a specific policy is in place. In this regard the sector shows maturity and does not obtain a lot of export business on the spot market. Exposure in terms of foreign currencies is concentrated, with the bulk of exports paid for in U.S. dollars. All the firms surveyed agreed that the truly significant exchange rate fluctuation is that of the *real* vis-à-vis the dollar, though one of the firms expressed concern about fluctuation against the deutsche mark.

The companies have learned a number of important lessons from exporting. In particular, more than one firm began acquiring technology by copying and then went on to develop its own technology and adapt it to exports. One firm surveyed had recourse to foreign designs. Moreover, given that foreign markets are more demanding in terms of quality control, exporting has led to significant improvements in quality. However, all the firms recognized that the domestic market has itself become more demanding in recent years. Certification is also important: one firm has certification by the main client, while the others have ISO 9000, QS 9000, and ISO 1400 certification.

Notwithstanding the multiple lessons learned through exporting, there was unanimous agreement that the red tape associated with exporting cuts profits. Firms learn a lot about such features as the need to have available local support and advanced technology skills. However, confronted by port and transport problems, the firms are obliged to find complex solutions to storing their merchandise.

One major difference between domestic and foreign markets that benefits sales in the domestic market are the demands of exporting in terms of quality, pricing, deadlines, and technical support. In addition, a closer relationship with large customers (automotive assembly firms) makes it possible to upgrade skills ranging from management to logistics, since, as one firm put it, "the cost of a product that is returned is huge in terms of its impact on the brand."

One of the questions that elicited the greatest degree of consensus was that concerning sources of competitiveness. The inquiry about whether the cost of labor was a source of competitiveness met with a unanimous response of "not any more." The same held true for inputs, which are no longer viewed as a source of competitiveness vis-à-vis foreign firms, and domestic financing. One aspect stressed was the supply of skilled labor, and especially the issue of whether it was adaptable and flexible enough to take on new functions in the factory. Two firms placed even greater emphasis on product differentiation. And, obviously, the exchange rate was perceived as the great villain of recent years.

There were no great surprises when it came to the requirements of the legal environment, the existence of unfair trade practices, and the importance of PTAs. One firm pointed to the low wages in China, India, and Poland as an example of unfair trade practices. All firms reported that they made little use of drawbacks, because of their complexity. The company executives stated that Mercosur had as yet generated little activity.

When asked what barriers were an obstacle for export growth, all firms singled out the same factors. First and foremost was the exchange rate, though two firms indicated that this will become a less significant problem over the long term (as the "Brazil cost" is brought down). Then there are the problems and challenges associated with infrastructure, especially ports and roads, in terms of their inefficiency and high costs, that constitute enormous obstacles; the complexity of the tax system; and the legal and regulatory frameworks, criticized for being corrupt and excessively bureaucratic (e.g., several documents being required for the same purpose). Certificates of origin for Mercosur differ from one country to the next. One respondent even felt that Brazil's negative image in some business forums hampers exports.

The textile industry. In Brazil's industrial profile the textile-manufacturing sector has been poorly represented in external markets. Up until just recently imports were insignificant. Even in spite of a big rise in synthetic and blended textile imports, they still supply only a small portion of the total market. Meanwhile, the domestic industry does not have a tradition of exporting: in fact, Brazil was a large-scale exporter of textiles only during World War II.

In contrast to the car parts firms, textile companies included in the study are not noted for very large export volumes, and essentially serve the domestic market.[30] They include a manufacturer whose main product is fabric for shirts made of 100% cotton with exports on the order of US$1.7 million, a manufacturer of fine textiles, and a maker of synthetic textiles primarily for packing sacks. Two of the firms have multiplant operations, with a high degree of vertical integration in production (close to 90%). This is in marked contrast to the production structure of the car parts sector. Of all the textile firms in our sample, only one had undertaken a generalized restructuring of production methods.

Exports amount to 10 to 15% of production capacity. Imports account for between 10 and 20% of the value of raw materials. One firm even imports raw cotton, a product that Brazil has traditionally exported. The reasons for this are the superior quality of the imported raw material and the financing terms for those imports, a common complaint by businesspeople in this industry.

All the firms have been operating for a considerable time in the domestic market, but have been involved only intermittently in exporting since they were established. One firm alone has exported products continuously since the late 1960s. For the others exporting is secondary to production for the domestic market: the companies do not have a strategy of investing specifically for export. Given the characteristics of textile production processes, investments may either be incremental or *en bloc*, depending on the product line (e.g., yarn, fabrics, garments).

Both dealers and trading companies are involved in the sales process, with a small portion of sales made directly through a firm's export department. None of the firms has its own offices or factories abroad, but some have entered into operating agreements. Mirroring the views of virtually all the others in the sample, these firms see attendance at trade fairs as vital for introducing products to clients.

In most cases competition is based on price. However, for the finest textiles competition is also based on product differentiation. These cases provide the best opportunities for boosting exports. The exporting strategy, where one exists, is based on exporting a set portion of total production as the main way of maintaining a minimal, stable share in export markets. As with the other firms surveyed, fluctuations in the exchange rate are a major factor, given that the bulk of exports go to countries with whom trade is negotiated in U.S. dollars. One of the firms pointed out that exchange rate considerations carry enormous weight in negotiations with foreign customers.

Exposure to the world market provides an opportunity for constant learning. For instance, exporters take advantage of visits to trade fairs and exhibitions to seek out the information they need to renew styles and patterns for both domestic and foreign markets. However, it is the domestic market that exporters have in mind. Some firms hire consultants or designers, while others simply copy the trends observed abroad in order to sell to both markets. Clearly, product design gives a boost to exporting, which requires stricter quality control that in turn steers firms to a learning process, whose results are reflected in domestic sales. One firm indicated that quality control was the same for both markets. None felt there was a need for certification in either case, nor for ISO certification.

With respect to transport logistics the findings of the study were varied. One of the firms uses FOB contracts, thus making the customer assume responsibility for all aspects of transport. The firm in question even exports by air. Other firms also send small cargoes by this means. Technical assistance is less important in this sector than in others, though all firms stated that they provide such assistance on an ongoing basis.

In contrast with other sectors, the sources of competitiveness emphasized here are labor and the exchange rate. However, product differentiation is also of greater importance: all firms indicated this factor as the major source of competitiveness. Financing arrangements are a potential source of competitiveness, especially since textile imports are now accompanied by foreign supplier credit provided under extremely favorable terms.

The main barriers faced by exports include, above all, the exchange rate; a lack of sufficient and appropriate export financing; high nonwage labor costs (on the order of 100% of the wage bill); port costs (primarily at the port of Santos, São Paulo State); and the high financial cost of loans in the domestic market. Some of these issues have come under government attention. In any event, it is unlikely that significant progress can soon be made in the infrastructure reform required to reduce the cost of exporting from Brazil or in reforms to the Brazilian federal constitution.

The pulp and paper industry. Out of the four industries chosen for the present investigation, the pulp and paper industry presents the greatest degree of heterogeneity in terms of product range (even taking into account the capital goods segment, which is characterized by a wide range of technologies and type of product). The sector contains one large integrated firm manufacturing pulp and printing and writing paper in rolls—set up specifically with exporting in mind—a semi-integrated medium-sized firm producing reams for writing and printing, and a small firm producing specialty paper. The problems of such diverse firms are to a certain extent dissimilar. However, as we shall see, there are marked similarities in some aspects.

The firm of Bahía Sur, which has a plant in Mucuri, in Bahía State, manufactures pulp fiber from eucalyptus trees on its own plantation. This is a huge integrated venture, which started operating only recently. Roughly 40% of its nominal capacity of 500,000 tons of pulp are used to manufacture paper, with the rest sold as is.[31] Close to 80% of pulp is exported, which means that the firm's revenues depend substantially on trends in overseas prices, which fluctuate markedly over time, and the exchange rate. Still, the firm has almost 40% of the domestic market for the type of paper it manufactures.

The industry has a complete vertical integration. Subcontracting is concentrated in forestry services and is nonexistent in manufacturing proper. One recent development is the outsourcing of some services in such areas as security and cleaning. Levels of utilization of installed capacity are high (above 90%), as one would expect in projects of this nature. Neither raw materials nor any other sorts of materials are imported.

The project has had an export orientation since its conception in 1985. Operations began in 1988, and vertical integration of paper production dates from 1990. From then onward investments were made specifically with a view to exporting; manufacturing paper was one way of adding value to the production process. This objective is shared by a range of large pulp-manufacturing firms.

Pirahy, a medium-sized firm, has a small presence in both domestic and foreign markets. Vertical integration is relatively advanced, except in the case of pulp, which is acquired from third parties, always in Brazil. Meanwhile, Daru imports almost all raw materials, in particular paper, for quality reasons. Technological modernization is an ongoing feature.

Most equipment is produced domestically, especially in paper manufacture, though this is not the case for specialty paper. The digester for the manufacture of cellulose pulp is imported. The nature of the production process is such that it is possible to carry out marginal investments in the manufacture of various types of paper, but not in manufacturing pulp.

Agreements to supply large customers with exports take the form of commitment letters. The use of trading companies for sales and marketing is not common. Large firms are the exception, since they have their own trading companies. In contrast to the other sectors already analyzed, pulp and paper firms do not regard attendance at trade fairs and exhibitions either in Brazil or abroad as particularly relevant. One important aspect of this sector's competitiveness is the reliability in the supply of products. For the specialty paper firm, differentiation in respect of the quality of the paper and precision is an important factor.

Pulp and paper firms were the first to highlight the issue of quality control and the need for certification, particularly for pulp exports to Europe. Foreign customers are more demanding in quality and deadlines. When asked about the export learning process, firms once again mentioned Brazil's excessive bureaucracy as regards standards and laws.

The sources of competitiveness alluded to show little variation from the cases examined above. Once again, the firms examined have reported that the advantage of cheap labor has disappeared in recent years. One of the specific features of this industry is that the wood used to manufacture pulp is a major source of competitive advantage. Another notable advantage has to do with the projects' being self-sufficient in energy.

Drawbacks are not especially relevant to the sector as a whole, since few inputs are imported. By contrast, the drawback mechanism figures prominently for the specialty paper firm because it mostly imports raw materials. Securitization of exports is a major form of financing for pulp and paper sales. This is not the case of specialty paper manufacturers, who tend to use advances on exchange contracts to finance production for export. The elimination of the state merchandise and service sales tax (ICMS), where applied to exports of semimanufactures, was seen as a boost to exports. The only country singled out for unfair trade practices was Indonesia, for engaging in dumping to penetrate pulp markets. And as for barriers to exports, firms alluded to the familiar set of factors, including, above all, the exchange rate slippage, deficient infrastructure (especially port facilities), and the lack of a specific export policy at the federal level. Respondents also pointed to the excessive proliferation of government bodies divided among different ministries as an obstacle to an effective export policy.

The machinery and equipment industry. The machinery and equipment industry suffered the most from the impact of trade liberalization in Brazil and the "strong *real*" policy of recent years.[32] In this industry, import penetration ratios (defined as imports' share of apparent consumption) now reach as much as 40 to 50% in some segments, compared with under 10% up until the late 1980s. Levels of idle capacity remain very high, quite similar to those seen during the recession of the 1980s.

Of all of Brazil's manufacturing industries, it is the capital goods sector as a whole that has lagged most in terms of technological modernization. Highly protected up until the late 1980s, the industry faced intense competition from imports by the mid-1990s. This competition was reinforced by supplier credits granted to imports under terms very favorable in contrast to those prevailing in Brazil.

This has been the panorama facing the firms selected for the study.[33] Companies have often engaged in exporting to take advantage of existing idle capacity. The exception was the firm that manufactures lathes—computer numerically controlled—that exports 30% of its output. For this firm, exporting is an important source of revenue and therefore is an integral part of the firm's strategy. This company accounts for 70% of Brazil's exports of lathes, as well as 40% of domestic sales.

The firms investigated are single-plant operations. Unlike as in almost all the other sectors, they have not made substantial changes to either management methods or subcontracting arrangements. Electronic equipment and components make up the bulk of imports. The firms surveyed have been in business for some years, with two of them approaching the 100-year mark. The firms are also vertically integrated.

The technological evolution in this sector, perhaps even more than in the textile-manufacturing sector, has encompassed all the classical stages of import substitution. Initially production catered to the domestic market. Later, mainly in the 1970s and 1980s, the sector recorded export growth, owing to either a devalued exchange rate, low capacity utilization, or specific export incentives for the export of manufactures (which were discontinued in the 1980s). Under this process, product lines were frequently changed to reflect demand requirements.

Investments are predominantly short-term in nature, and it is often possible to increase the scale of production with marginal, incremental investments. This should make it easier to adapt to new product lines. However, product line reorganizations have not been the prevailing trend among the firms surveyed.

Initially, products enjoyed the benefit of foreign know-how, often obtained by copying. In this sector, copying is not only an unpleasant reality, reflecting technological backwardness, but was the normal way of acquiring technology in the past. The situation is somewhat different today because there is some endogenous development of technology. Product design is conducted in-house by firms. There are no particular quality controls for exports, nor is it necessary to obtain certifications to export.

The problems involved in supplying technical assistance to potential customers pushed one firm to operate an assembly plant abroad—in Kentucky.

A variety of arrangements are used for the sales and marketing of exports; these range from subsidiaries in the United States and contracts in Europe (e.g., Ferrostaal) to designated agents (138 in the United States, in the case of Nardini), as well as dealers and trading companies. Firms emphasized the importance of participating in trade fairs, especially abroad.

The tradition of exporting is considered a source of competitiveness: hence the importance of providing technical assistance, complemented by product differentiation, and, to a lesser extent, by price competition. Exports go mainly to dollar countries and/or are sold in U.S.

dollars. One firm conducts business in deutsche marks. Clearly, then, the exchange rate fluctuation of most significance is that of the *real* in relation to the U.S. dollar.

One important part of the export learning process cited by two firms was dealing with bureaucracy.[34] There is still a huge amount of red tape associated with exporting.

Among the sources of competitiveness cited were these:

- Product differentiation, which is seen as fundamental.
- The supply of skills in terms of adaptability and flexibility for the execution of the most diverse tasks. Here again, it was stated that the cost of labor had ceased to be a source of competitiveness, as was borne out in all the other interviews, following the enactment of the 1988 constitution and the implementation of the *Real* Plan.

It is worth pointing out that the appreciating exchange rate has represented a not insubstantial competitive advantage for firms that import raw materials, equipment, and components on a large scale. However, even taking this into account, in the final analysis devaluation was judged necessary and urgent. Almost all the businesspeople surveyed believe that devaluation is also important to correct or counterbalance the competitive disadvantages generated by the high Brazil cost.

As was the case with all other sectors and businesses, managers in the machinery and equipment industry were unanimous in their criticism concerning (1) the lack of financing whose terms, amounts, and maturities were on a par with those enjoyed by competing imports and (2) the exchange rate lag. In addition, there were the usual complaints about problems experienced with ports (especially Santos, in São Paulo State), the excessive red tape associated with exporting, and the lack of an authentic export-import bank to provide export financing. None of the firms found useful the form of export financing made available by BNDES specifically for capital goods (i.e., FINAMEX). All the companies use or have used advances on exchange contracts or advances on export contracts.

Conclusions

The combination of a three-year recession (1990–1992) with a gradual process of trade liberalization—which was more clearly perceived by the productive sector and consumers from 1993 onwards—forced

Brazilian industry to rethink its production methods and change the thrust of its efforts to overhaul management and technological practices. These changes signaled a genuine turning point in the performance of the manufacturing sector. The course charted since that time is proof that expanded international trade linkages have a cost, but that they are vital to improving business competitiveness. Brazil, like so many other countries that underwent similar processes, is no exception to this rule.

The industrial structure and dynamic emerging from these processes have yet to be consolidated. Industries have demonstrated resiliency in the face of foreign competition. However, it is important to recognize the need to foster a new model of industrial development. It can be hoped that the defensive posture adopted by industry since the early 1990s is only a temporary response, since Brazil requires investment strategies that increase production capacity. The manufacturing industry has recently begun to show signs of adopting an "offensive" investment strategy. However, investments in manufacturing have not yet reached such a level that one can speak of the advent of a new model.

Meanwhile, some recent changes—notably a striking increase in the import penetration ratio in a number of sectors—indicate, given the size of domestic and foreign markets and Brazil's technological tradition, that the time is fast approaching when scale of production will justify investing in local manufacture of many goods that today are imported. At the same time, substantial productivity gains in industry, coupled with investment in production for export, will generate greater export sales than Brazil has recorded up until quite recently.

As repeatedly emphasized in this chapter, stabilization with the exchange rate anchor as part of the macroeconomic strategy of a strong *real* has brought about a relative appreciation of the exchange rate since mid-1994.[35] The microeconomic impact of macroeconomic policies should not be minimized: all the firms surveyed felt that the overvalued exchange rate was one of the main barriers to export growth. However, the more perceptive among them have now become aware that this state of things will change only gradually and that it is not possible to rely on significant devaluations of the exchange rate as an element of external competitiveness in the short run. In this regard, recent foreign exchange policy has been one of small devaluations ahead of wholesale industrial goods' price increases. Moreover, this policy has in its favor huge productivity gains.[36]

Continuing high interest rates are a second macroeconomic factor noted in interviews. The combination of a hitherto insufficient fiscal adjustment, the need to attract foreign capital in order to finance the domestic account, and the need to monitor the growth in credit (which could overheat demand to excessive levels) has led to very high *real* interest rates, and that has discouraged productive investment. Interest rates are trending downward gradually, as efforts are made to reduce public-sector deficits by a variety of means.

The forms of financing available to industry are perceived as being very expensive. It is worth noting that the National Bank for Economic and Social Development (BNDES) has recently announced measures aimed at improving export financing.[37] The initiatives by the bank have up until quite recently not been well received by exporting firms: in fact, not one of the firms surveyed accorded any importance to those forms of financing. The inadequacy of export financing was another significant factor alluded to in the course of the interviews.

Mention should also be made of the advances in exchange contracts and the advances in export contracts already described briefly. These mechanisms will no doubt tend to lose importance over the medium and long term, as nominal domestic interest rates start to align themselves with rates prevailing internationally (after considering exchange rate devaluation and a Brazil risk premium).

One of the most surprising facts to come out of the study has to do with sources of competitiveness. In this regard, labor received a special mention. Nonwage labor costs that amount to nearly 100% of the wage bill, thus comprising one of the main components of the Brazil cost, pose a major burden. In addition, the wages of industrial labor (i.e., the product wage) have consistently risen in real terms from the beginning of the 1990s to mid-1996; their growth has even outpaced the huge productivity gains recorded by industry, as evidenced by wages' increased share of the value of production. With a strong exchange rate, the cost burden imposed by the labor expense component reduces profit margins and accelerates the cut in the use of labor.[38] In this manner, Brazil has recently lost what should have been one of its potential sources of competitiveness: the low cost of labor.

One positive aspect noted about the labor force pertains to its quality. A number of those interviewed referred to this and underlined the ease of learning, the positive capacity for improvising and seeking solutions for problems and related issues—in Portuguese, *jeitinho brasileiro*. This is surprising, in view of the low average level of *formal* qualifications of workers in Brazil's industry. Hence this factor should be considered as a major source of competitiveness.

All those surveyed agreed that there was too much interference and red tape associated with exporting. Several of the interviews were notable for frequent criticism about the excessive number of forms required and of regulations.

The bureaucracy that has sprung up to harness the benefits of free-trade agreements (Mercosur) also came in for harsh criticism. There were problems with the issuing of certificates of origin and the preparation of declarations of origin, because norms varied from one member nation to the next.

The proliferation of government agencies divided among a range of ministries is also an obstacle to exporting: there needs to be a single authority. The lack of a foreign trade policy formulated at the federal level was also stressed. Initiatives at the state level, for their part, have much more to do with attracting firms to the respective regions than with providing support and incentives to export.

Predictably, business people complained about the high cost and inefficiencies of port systems, in particular, as well as of road and rail transport systems. Some in business were in favor of the privatization initiatives undertaken in those areas, but all expressed doubts concerning the results of privatizations and new concessions over the medium term.

As for their contacts with customers, firms declared that it was very useful to make regular visits to countries where they had distributors, in those cases when they did not have their own offices abroad. Likewise, and taking into account potential customers, *all the firms,* irrespective of their size and field of activity, underlined the importance of attending foreign trade fairs.

Economic policy recommendations that can be made on the basis of the conclusions drawn are all relatively straightforward. The difficulty lies in actually implementing them. Thus complaints about the appreciating exchange rate, so frequent in public statements by exporters, have recently begun to lose weight: (1) the Brazilian government frequently reaffirms its foreign exchange policy; and (2) in practice, the government undertakes discrete *real* devaluations in the exchange rate, particularly in relation to market prices for industrial goods. The aim of the government over the short and medium term is to reduce the Brazil cost as a way of boosting the profitability of exports.

However, the most feasible way of expanding exports is in the area of financing and related items (e.g., credit insurance, financing extended to importers of Brazilian products). For at least the past three years, there has been discussion about the need to set up an export-import bank to promote exports. Some time ago, the BNDES announced that it intended to expand its role in this sphere, even focusing on activities typically undertaken by an export-import bank, though the BNDES has only been partially successful up to now. This, however, is not something that can be achieved overnight. The lack of a tradition in this area and in others generates frustration and disenchantment in business circles.

The main difficulties in the area of export financing come from the fact that the task of supplying credit is split among a number of government agencies. Besides, there is uncertainty over budgetary allocations for equalization of interest rates. Furthermore, the rules governing private-sector operations are not entirely stable. Export insurance has existed for quite some time but has never functioned satisfactorily, owing to inadequate management of commercial and political risks, combined with overestimates of compensation by claimants. The system is currently under review.

The key issue concerns the funding of exports, not only in terms of the rates and conditions applied to loans, but also of the amounts required in a country the size, and with the exporting tradition, of Brazil. Turning to overseas sources for financing may prove an interim solution while the fiscal adjustment is worked through and domestic interest rates decline. Even then, it would be necessary to envisage a review fee of a small (or nil) amount to make loans attractive.

On the other hand, it is somewhat naive to believe that in the current phase of Brazil's stabilization effort, the National Treasury can finance the cost of interest rate equalization on a sufficient scale to promote exports (and deny promotion to many competing industries, ranging from housing finance to agriculture, for example) in a country where the consolidated government operating deficit is currently on the order of 5% of GDP.

Similarly, it is essential to invest in production to encourage exports, and not just in the sale and marketing of exportable products. There is recognition that various product lines were not accompanied by investments in the past. In view of the time it takes for investments to bear fruit, there is always a lag before any appreciable growth occurs in export sales. Moreover, the terms of financing for those new investments run up against the same difficulties mentioned above in relation to investments in sales and marketing. Consequently, it is very difficult to come up with short-term solutions.

It is necessary to stress again the importance placed by virtually all respondents on a versatile, flexible labor force as a source of competitiveness. In fact, in several cases, this was the only *positive* factor of competitiveness reported by those surveyed for the study.[39] It is difficult to imagine how a policy can be formulated to expand or reinforce this factor—apparently intrinsic and connected, perhaps, to more permanent cultural traits of Brazil's labor force. How can this positive aspect of industrial labor be encouraged? That question is beyond the scope of this chapter. In the meantime, hopes are that an improvement in the level of formal schooling of the labor force—very low in Brazil, as in other countries of Latin America—will help enhance further these traits of flexibility and versatility.

During the investigation, the need for Brazil to have a more explicit foreign trade policy was clearly identified. Such a policy should, of course, offer viable alternatives for shaping what could and should be Brazil's export future within the framework of the new economic policy regime that has emerged since the stabilization plan was launched.

This policy should, at a minimum, do the following:

1. Clearly define the *objectives and instruments* of Brazil's foreign trade policy, particularly in relation to exports
2. As part of these instruments, emphasize the role of *financing production for export and financing the sales and marketing* of exportable products
3. Provide for clear linkages to *industrial policy, technology policy,* and measures to reduce the Brazil cost
4. Centralize in *one or a small number of institutions* the task of administering instruments and measures
5. Take steps to *reduce the bureaucracy* associated with foreign trade activities and implement measures aimed at simplifying the bureaucratic procedures involved in exporting,[40] (notwithstanding the considerable improvement noted since September 1992, when the export module of the computerized integrated foreign trade system [SICOMEX] came into operation)[41]
6. Ensure stable rules of the game
7. Promote participation in trade fairs and exhibitions in Brazil, and especially abroad, by providing logistical and financial assistance for firms[42]
8. Seek out means and methods of fostering a versatile and flexible industrial labor force because this factor is particularly pertinent from the standpoint of competitiveness and was emphasized in several interviews

Notes

1. Exports of goods FOB only rose from US$45.5 billion to US$47.7 billion between 1995 and 1996.

2. Obviously that distinction is merely academic. Note that the balance of payments was not affected by the trade deficits incurred in 1995 and 1996, due to the willingness to receive inflows of capital from abroad and loans. The latter were attracted by the high differential between domestic and external interest rates, especially in 1995, as well as in 1996.

3. The information used for this chapter comes from different sources. Therefore there may be discrepancies.

4. Parts of this section are based on A. C. Pinheiro (1996). The Brazilian Geographical and Statistical Institute (IBGE) and the Central Bank provided the information, especially that pertaining to the national accounts of Brazil.

5. See E. Bacha (1995) and (1996).

6. Ibid. p.3.

7. For purposes of comparison, if Brazil had maintained the share of world exports it had in 1979, in 1995 exports would have totaled US$72.6 billion, some 60% above the level actually recorded in 1995 (US$45.5 billion).

8. One example shows the role of the exchange rate: in 1995 the value of Brazil's exports to Japan rose by 20.5%, and the main reason was the appreciation of the yen in that year.

9. This schedule was speeded up in February 1992, and again in 1994.

10. In fact, the schedule was not altered. It was the tariff rates in force in the schedule's completion that changed. Tariff reductions were brought forward by three months in line with Mercosur, and, given that rates were modified only slightly, the only effect felt was in terms of expectations, and not on the competitiveness of local products.

11. Earlier experience with export promotion mechanisms such as BEFIEX and FINEX turned out to be disastrous due to inefficiency, corruption, the high level of subsidies and the drain on public finances. This probably explains why the issue has of late been treated with caution and why the economic authorities have been reluctant to adopt more comprehensive initiatives at a time when all efforts are focused on dealing with the fiscal situation and the trade balance.

12. In addition to the instruments mentioned in the text, there are others less widely used, temporarily not in use, or specific to certain sectors (e.g., agriculture): exchange debentures, commodities lines, forfeiting (forward sales, capital goods, and promissory notes), and warrant discounts, among others. An analytical description of these mechanisms can be found in E. Fortuna (1994).

13. See Bonelli (1997) for a thorough description of these instruments.

14. In its initial phase of operation, up until 1995, the program was plagued by problems and represented a considerable cost for public finances and hence was rarely used.

15. Note that because of this (and the high differential between domestic and foreign interest rates at the outset of the *Real* Plan, with a progressive appreciation of the exchange rate), it became common practice to take resources from advances on exchange contracts and invest them at market rates. This practice was subsequently discontinued.

16. Information provided by the Central Bank of Brazil; exports paid for in advance accounted for 13.6% of total exports in 1994 and 1995 and around 20.0% in the first half of 1996.

17. This type of loan has been termed "exporters' 63," in reference to Central Bank Resolution 63, which regulates the inflow of funds for loans both by commercial and investment banks.

18. In fact, the decree regulates Law 6704 of 26 October 1979.

19. According to estimates by the National Confederation of Industry, basic social costs of industrial labor amount to 102% of wages! These are the mandatory expenses for hiring a worker in industry, a little over twice the contractual wage. This issue was constantly referred to in the interviews conducted with business people.

20. Apart from stimulating industrial investments, this agreement also contributed to a reduction in the Brazil cost, since it reduced the tax on exports of capital goods and raw materials, thus allowing a drop in the fiscal costs of investment.

21. After coming to power, the current administration enacted Law 9000/95 on 16 March 1995, which increased the list of exemptions from the industrial products tax (IPI) to include purchases of a range of capital goods—machinery, equipment, new devices and instruments, both imported and made in Brazil, as well as the respective accessories, especially tools—thus initiating the first steps toward reducing the fiscal cost of investments. This law remained in force until 31 December 1995, with the exemptions to the IPI kept in place thanks to temporary measures.

22. With the exception of the first two activities listed in the table, agriculture and mining, these activities comprise manufacturing industry.

23. The penetration of imports of synthetic and blended textiles (especially from South Korea and China) has been so intense that it caused the shutdown of entire regional segments, such as the textile center in the city of Americana in São Paulo. There roughly half the factories set up before 1990 closed their doors. As a general rule it was the oldest textile-producing plants that were the hardest hit. The bulk of textile production is made up of blended synthetic and natural fabrics.

24. For example, COFAP has 72% of the domestic market in shock absorbers and 81% in rings. It also accounts for 85% of all shock absorbers and 90% of rings exported by Brazil. Metal Leve has 60% of the domestic market in pistons—90% in bronze parts and 50% in plastic parts. Its share of the export market is 50% for pistons, 100% for bronze parts, and 50% for plastic parts. SABO has roughly two-thirds of the domestic market in retainers, and both companies have a 35% share of hoses.

25. Metal Leve has four plants in Brazil and three abroad; COFAP has eight in Brazil and one abroad, while SABO has three in Brazil and four abroad (including one in Buenos Aires). Some plants are operated in association with foreign firms. In December 1996 COFAP announced plans to open two additional plants in 1997, worth US$40 million each: one in Argentina and one in the United States.

26. Metal Leve exports 40% of its production capacity in pistons—20% in bronze parts and 10–15% in plastic parts. COFAP exports 50% of its production capacity in shock absorbers and 45% in rings, while SABO exports 30% of its capacity in retainers and 15% in connection tubes and hoses.

27. Metal Leve began production of pistons in 1950, diversifying into bronze parts in 1956–1957. Plastic parts only began to be produced in 1976. COFAP started producing rings in 1951–1953, which grew with the export of blocks, and after 1970 began exporting rings.

28. Metal Leve was fairly different in a number of ways. The firm began exporting to other Latin American countries at the beginning of the 1960s, having made investments for that specific purpose. At the end of the 1960s, Metal Leve carried out investments with a view to exporting diesel and airplane engines to the

North American market. It was only in the 1970s that the company took conscious steps to invest in the production of pistons for export.

29. One of the firms manages to sell about two-thirds of its exports to captive clients, with the remainder going to the spare parts market through representatives and distributors.

30. Ferreira Guimares holds 45% of the domestic market for dyed knitwear and prints and 40% for light and heavy indigos. Nova America has 35% of the domestic market for fabric for shirts.

31. Annual production of printing and writing paper in rolls amounts to around 180,000 tons.

32. Exports of capital goods, including parts, components, and accessories, typically reached US$3–4 billion a year not too long ago. Recently, exports have not exceeded US$3 billion, and their share of total exports has declined.

33. Thus in the case of one firm, exports dropped from around US$25 million in the mid-1980s to under US$17 million in 1995. Another firm even recorded nil exports in some years.

34. It needs to be recognized that this is an extremely negative aspect: the main lesson learned from exporting is how to cope with excessive bureaucracy.

35. It would not be appropriate to spell out the huge variety of measurements, each featuring a different price index, that have been used to estimate Brazil's "exchange rate lag." Apparently independent measurements prepared by the employers association CNI (Confederação Nacional de Indústria)—using the real exchange rate for industrial products—show that between June 1994 and December 1996, the exchange rate had appreciated by roughly 6 to 8%.

36. According to estimates based on gross real industrial production, labor productivity has increased on the average by about 7.5% per annum between 1990 and 1995. Estimates for the year under way point to a similar figure, with indications that it may even go higher. These productivity gains clearly occurred with less domestic value added than before, given the growth in imports of component parts that followed liberalization. In addition, major job losses were noted in industry, though most were due to the recession of 1990–1992.

37. In late 1996, the bank announced its intention to guarantee exports financed by importers of Brazilian products abroad. A group of foreign banks were to receive accreditation to act as agents, operating with transfers of its credit lines.

38. It is highly significant that when asked in the survey whether labor was an important factor of competitiveness, almost all the firms replied "not any more."

39. The degree of unanimity on the importance of this factor is somewhat surprising.

40. All Brazilian exporters are required to register with the Department of Foreign Trade, at the Ministry of Industry, Commerce, and Tourism.

41. The system uses a single export record for most products. Exceptions include exports financed at terms of over 180 days. The terms require a document detailing a record of a loan and a number of products selected for ecological or strategic reasons, which require a special authorization.

42. The BNDES operates a scheme to provide financial assistance for trade fairs and exhibitions. However, this line of funding is rarely used, perhaps because firms are unaware of its existence.

5

Colombia: Regaining the Upper Hand in Export Promotion

Carla Macario

Colombia was the first country in Latin America to establish a coherent set of export promotion policies in the late 1960s. The nation became a model for the other countries in the region that were attempting to design efficient export assistance policies. Therefore, it was essential to include it in the project that assessed the impact of export promotion policies on the behavior of export firms.[1]

The Macroeconomic Environment

The Colombian economy grew at a rate of 0.7% in 1998. The country is one of the mid-sized economies in Latin America—along with Chile, Peru, and Venezuela—with a GDP of US$84 billion (at 1995 prices) in 1998 (see Table 5.1).[2]

The country's macroeconomic stability during the 1980s was outstanding when compared with that of other Latin American nations. This allowed Colombia to have an annual average rate of growth of per capita GDP of 1.6%, while many other countries in the region ended the decade with lower levels than in 1980.

Manufacturing's share of GDP was 18.4% for 1997, down from 20.8% in 1990. Industrial output, excluding coffee processing, has grown at a rate of 6.7% between January and June 1998 (DANE 1998c).

Colombia exported US$14.7 billion of goods and services in 1998, while imports were US$18 billion. Imports of goods and services were 21.6% of GDP in 1998, more than twice as much as in 1990 before the trade liberalization reforms. In contrast, exports' share of GDP has only increased from 13.3 to 17.5% over the same period. The country's

Table 5.1 Colombia: Economic Indicators

	1990	1991	1992	1993	1994	1995	1996	1997	1998[g]
GDP[a]	65,028	66,100	68,662	71,740	76,245	80,400	82,058	83,310	83,904
GDP growth rates[b]	3.3	1.6	3.9	4.5	6.3	5.4	2.1	1.5	0.7
Imports[a,c]	5,776	5,972	8,439	11,706	14,373	15,825	16,299	18,019	18,097
Exports[a,c]	8,634	9,669	10,212	10,885	10,852	12,144	12,679	13,477	14,662
Import ratio[d]	8.9	9.0	12.3	16.3	18.9	19.7	19.9	21.6	21.6
Export ratio (all goods)[d]	13.3	14.6	14.9	15.2	14.2	15.1	15.5	16.2	17.5
Export ratio (manufactures)[e]	25.1	33.3	31.8	39.9	36.9	38.0	33.6	30.7	32.2
Exchange rate[f]	502	633	679	787	827	913	1,037	1,141	1,426

Source: ECLAC, on the basis of official figures.
a. Millions of U.S. dollars at 1995 prices.
b. Average annual rates at 1995 prices.
c. Goods and services.
d. Percentages of GDP at 1995 prices. Includes goods and services.
e. Percentages of total value of FOB exports of goods.
f. Nominal exchange rate in pesos per U.S. dollar.
g. Preliminary figures.
Information is from different sources, so there may be discrepancies.

degree of openness (the sum of imports and exports over GDP) was 39.1% in 1998 compared to 22.2% in 1990, an increase that is mainly due to import growth.

Colombia's main export product is crude petroleum (20.3% of exports in 1997). Oil has replaced coffee as the country's chief export product. Coffee's share of exports has gone from 49.1% in 1985 to 19.6% in 1997.

The rise and fall of the price of coffee in international markets was for many years the main determinant of the availability of hard currency. Therefore it had a strong impact on the domestic business cycle. In consequence, the growing importance of oil has diversified the country's exports and has decreased the economy's vulnerability to the fluctuations of the price of coffee. Nevertheless, there is now a greater exposure to the variations of the oil market. After oil and coffee, the next leading exports are coal (7.6%), cut flowers (4.7%), fresh bananas (4.4%), and oil products (3.2%).

Export growth during the first half of the 1990s was mainly the result of an increase of nontraditional exports, which increased by 37% between 1991 and 1995. The main nontraditional exports are textiles, chemical products, emeralds, bananas, and flowers (OMC 1997b).

Export performance has been dampened by the appreciation of the exchange rate during the 1990s as a result, among other factors, of the discoveries of new oil fields. Over this period, the Colombian peso has appreciated against the currencies of most of its trading partners, with the exception of Argentina and, to a lesser extent, of Venezuela (DANE 1998a). This appreciation of the Colombian peso has been somewhat compensated for by its recent devaluation following the economic turbulence in Asia. Nevertheless, there has been a major appreciation of the peso with respect to the currencies of such Asian countries as South Korea, Malaysia, and Thailand, which are among Colombia's chief rivals on the export markets for manufactured goods. This, along with the decrease of demand in Latin American countries, contributed to a decrease of exports during 1998 as compared to the same period during the previous year (–6.38%), while nontraditional exports grew by a modest 0.7% (DANE 1999b).

Trade Policy

Colombia adopted import substitution policies in the 1930s. These were combined with export promotion programs two decades later. While the intensity of these policies varied throughout the years, partly as a result of the fluctuations of the price of coffee, this "mixed strategy" was successful in stimulating export growth and diversification. This combination of policies also contributed to consolidating the manufacturing sector.

In 1967, the government's resolve to adopt a new set of policies contributed to providing the mixed strategy with a more coherent framework (Ocampo 1994). These included new export promotion policies that were a model for the other countries in Latin America (see below). The reforms were very successful and led to unprecedented high growth rates and export diversification during the late 1960s and early 1970s, a period that is known as Colombia's golden age.

All the same, the policies in place also led to very high effective rates of protection for some consumer goods industries, such as textiles, clothing, and footwear. Moreover, these policies were combined with widely scattered tariff levels and a predominance of nontariff barriers, therefore increasing the level of protection. At the same time, short-term macroeconomic goals often had a more decisive influence on trade policy than long-term development goals (Garay et al. 1998).

By the late 1980s and early 1990s, the decrease in the rates of growth and the shift in the policy environment in Latin America had led the Colombian government to abandon the mixed model and replace it by an outward oriented strategy (Ocampo and Villar 1995). This new strategy included changes of the trade policy, tax reform, and greater flexibility in exchange controls (Pardo 1996).

The main changes in trade policy were the following: the average nominal tariff—which had already been substantially cut during the previous years from 41.7% in 1984—went down from 26.6% in 1989 to 6.1% in 1991 (Ocampo 1994). The proportion of imports that required prior licensing went from 60.1% in 1989 to 1.4% in 1991 (Garay et al. 1998).

At present, tariffs go from 0% to 35%. The average tariff is 11.5% and the maximum tariff binding at the WTO for nonagricultural products is 35% (OMC 1997b).

Regional integration, through preferential trade agreements, has been a key goal of Colombia's trade policy. Colombia belongs to the Comunidad Andina (the former Grupo Andino) since it was established by that country together with Bolivia, Ecuador, Peru, and Venezuela in 1969. The purpose of the Comunidad Andina is to provide a larger market, particularly for manufactured goods. Around 20% of the country's exports go to the Comunidad Andina, and almost half of these are exports to Venezuela.

Colombia also has had a specific trade agreement with Venezuela since 1992. Trade between the two countries went up from US$1.0 billion in 1992 to more than US$2.5 billion in 1997.[3] This agreement provides Colombia with an opportunity to export goods with greater value added, since 80% of the country's exports to Venezuela are manufactured goods (Pardo 1996).

Colombia has a preferential trade agreement with Mexico within the framework of the agreement between the two and Venezuela—also known as the G-3—that took effect in January 1995. Colombia has also negotiated preferential tariffs with the Mercosur countries, that is Argentina, Brazil, Uruguay, and Paraguay. An agreement with Chile, which took effect in January 1994, reduced tariffs to zero for over 70% of the tariff items by 1997. The country also has agreements with the Caribbean Community and Common Market and with the countries of the Central American Common Market.

Colombian exports are granted tariff preferences in the United States and in Europe under several programs, which range from the Generalized System of Preferences to special programs that seek to encourage export diversification in countries in which illegal drug traffic originates.

Export Promotion Policies

Colombia's export promotion policy originates in Decree 444 of the 1967 reform aimed at designing a comprehensive strategy based on the following instruments: Proexpo, the country's export promotion agency and an instrument that grants a tax credit to exporters, the Certificado de Abono Tributario (CAT). At the same time the Plan Vallejo, a scheme allowing firms to be exempted from duties on imported inputs that had been in operation since 1961, was expanded.[4] These reforms made the country a forerunner in export promotion.

The main purpose of Proexpo was to provide firms with support for marketing abroad and with export credit, and was very effective. Therefore, it became a model for other Latin American and Caribbean countries that set up trade promotion organizations (TPOs). For instance, ProChile—the Chilean TPO—was designed using Proexpo as a benchmark.

The changes in trade policy carried out during the early 1990s also included reforms directly related to export promotion, such as the establishment of a ministry in charge of trade, the Ministerio de Comercio Exterior. At that moment, Proexpo was replaced by two different agencies: BANCOLDEX, the foreign trade bank, and Proexport, responsible for trade promotion. While the original law stated that the Ministerio de Comercio Exterior would be in charge of customs, this was not put in practice and operating customs became in fact the responsibility of the Finance Ministry, the Secretaría de Hacienda.[5]

Proexport was set up as a trust fund to allow a greater flexibility and autonomy than the standard public-sector agency. Proexport's programs provide exporters with support for marketing abroad under a cost-sharing arrangement. Most of these programs are based on the Unidades Exportadoras, small groups of entrepreneurs that export similar goods. In 1996, 100 Unidades Exportadoras were in operation, coordinating the export activity of 556 firms (OMC 1997b). Proexport's 1999 budget is approximately US$26 million, of which US$10 million will be used for trade promotion activities and US$13 million to cover operating expenses.[6]

BANCOLDEX provides export credit for domestic exporters and loans for importers of Colombian goods abroad. The trade bank provides loans at rates that are no longer subsidized. The bank is linked to the Ministerio de Comercio Exterior. It operates as a second-tier financial institution that channels its funds through commercial banks, and has recently set up an office to ensure that small and medium-size exporters have access to its loans (Ochoa 1998).

The export bank provides financing in pesos and in dollars for pre- and postshipment working capital, and for investment and industrial restructuring. Almost 80% of the loans provided by the bank in 1996 went to manufacturing firms, mainly from the textile and food-processing industries (Garay et al. 1998). In 1998, BANCOLDEX provided loans for a total of US$889 million to 529 large firms, US$146 million to 581 small and medium-sized firms, and US$59 million to 114 very small firms. Firms exporting nontraditional goods received 95% of these funds.[7]

The CAT set up by the 1967 reform was replaced by the Certificado de Reembolso Tributario (CERT) with the goal of increasing its effectiveness. The CERT, in operation since 1984, allows exporters of nontraditional goods a tax credit equivalent to a given percentage of the FOB value of the exported goods.[8] The purpose of this scheme is to reimburse an equivalent of the amount paid by exporters on tariffs and domestic indirect taxes. It is also aimed at offsetting the added costs entrepreneurs face when exporting from Colombia, such as those for infrastructure.

Exporters using the CERT can get a tax credit of 2.25%, 3.6%, or 4.5% of the FOB value, depending on the product and the country being exported to. In 1995, 2,577 tariff items could benefit from this instrument. The funds used for the CERT in 1996 were estimated at US$93 million. It was used by around 30% of the country's exports between 1992 and 1994. Banana and flower exports were the two main products that used the CERT over that period (OMC 1997b). The percentages of the FOB value refunded as a tax credit and the criteria used for applying the different levels have varied throughout the years.

The Plan Vallejo (also known as Sistemas Especiales de Importación-Exportación, or SIEX), allows companies exemption from part or all taxes on inputs, equipment, and spare parts used to manufacture exports or goods to be used in manufacturing exports. In the case of equipment and spare parts 70% of output has to be for export. For raw materials all of the output has to be exported.

Exports using this instrument accounted for 38.5% of total exports in 1995. Coal and agricultural goods were the main products benefiting from this scheme between 1993 and 1996. The share of nontraditional exports that used the Plan Vallejo was 58% between 1991 and 1995 (Garay et al. 1998).

Although they were established to offset the taxes paid by exports, the CERT and the Plan Vallejo have a subsidy component. Therefore they will have to be modified or phased out—for nonagricultural products—at the latest by 2003 to fulfill the country's commitments to the Uruguay Round Agreements.

Phasing out or eliminating the CERT and the Plan Vallejo will undoubtedly have negative consequences for export performance in the short run. The evidence presented above demonstrates that a significant share of exports uses these instruments. The research in successful export firms confirms this evidence (see below).

However, these schemes do not appear to contribute to an increase of export diversification at present: the funds allocated through these instruments are very concentrated on a few products. Moreover, there does not seem to have been an important change in the main products exported through the Plan Vallejo between 1985 and 1995 (Garay et al. 1998).

The subsidy component of Colombia's export promotion instruments led the United States to investigate the country's exports in the early 1980s. These investigations were suspended after the two countries resolved that Colombian exports going to the United States would not benefit from the CERT, from export loans at preferential rates, or from the Plan Vallejo (Garay et al. 1998).

At present, the Pastrana administration has announced that increasing exports (specifically manufactured exports) will be the uppermost priority for the government. With that goal in mind, it has been decided to reorganize Proexport by focusing most of its services on firms that are highly committed to exporting. Meanwhile, Proexport will continue providing information and trade fair support to a larger number of firms. At the same time, the trade promotion organization has been structured in units according to sectors (agricultural, manufacturing, clothing, and service industries).[9]

The government has also announced the elimination of the CERT for nonagricultural products, with the goal of complying with the country's commitments with the Uruguay Round Agreements (DANE 1998b). The funds presently used for the CERT for nonagricultural products will go to productivity enhancement programs that will be channeled through a special fund set up for that purpose, the Fondo de Productividad y Competitividad. The Plan Vallejo will be maintained for inputs and will therefore be phased out for equipment.[10]

At the same time, the Pastrana administration has presented a new program for increasing exports of goods with higher value added (Consejo Superior de Comercio Exterior 1998). This program includes numerous measures aimed at increasing productivity and decreasing export obstacles. It calls for an improved coordination among the different government agencies responsible for programs in the fields that have the potential for a strong impact on productivity. The main fields are innovation and technology, education and training, and assistance for small and medium-size export firms. The program also seeks to favor regional export strategies and to encourage foreign investment in high-value-added industries.

Firms' Export Behavior

The findings of research in export firms in Colombia are presented here. The issues addressed were the following. Which are the main factors that lead firms to export? Is there a learning process when companies export? If there is such a learning process, does it only take place in matters directly related to the export activity or does it have a larger scope? Are the export promotion instruments useful or not? Which are the main export obstacles? What is the influence of PTAs on companies' export opportunities? These issues were selected because of their importance for designing and assessing export promotion policies.

The twenty-one firms included in the study belong to the printing, leather products (mainly luggage and leather footwear), textiles, clothing, and food processing industries.[11] These industries were picked because they were among the top exporters of manufactured products with relatively high levels of value added.[12] One other firm, a software producer, was included in the survey because it is a growing, although small, export business in Latin America. Most of the companies are large by Latin American standards, at least in terms of the number of employees. Two of the firms were located in Cali, seven in Medellín, and the rest in Bogotá.

The interviews with executives of export firms were supplemented by others with representatives of trade associations. Government officials also provided information. The research in the Colombian firms was done at the end of 1995.

Main Factors Influencing Firms' Export Decisions

Companies decide to start exporting because it allows them to manufacture on a larger scale. Secondly, existing excess capacity can be used that could not otherwise be absorbed by the domestic market, given the firm's share in it. These two reasons may appear closely related, but they are different in that making better use of installed capacity is not the same thing as increasing the scale of the plant to take better advantage of long-run economies of scale.

The third reason that compels a company to export is the need to achieve a scale that allows it to preserve market share in the domestic market. This factor is related to the first two motives. However, there is a difference in that the company has to invest in upgrading its technology to protect its share of the domestic market from growing competition, particularly from imports. These new technologies often entail a volume of manufacturing output larger than the firm's share in the domestic market.

For instance, one of the clothing firms in the study in Medellín had to upgrade its technology so as to manufacture higher quality products to preserve its share of the domestic market. The technology upgrade in turn implied a larger scale of production, which therefore led the firm to try to export.

Hence there is a link between exporting and economies of scale. To improve their ability to face import competition, firms shift their production function. Doing so forces entrepreneurs to look for larger markets, and thus to export. This demonstrates that in the case of relatively small economies, exporting allows firms to achieve economies of scale that could not be possible when manufacturing only for the domestic market.

The proportion of exports when compared with the companies' total output was widely scattered. This was true irrespective of the industry. However, there is a threshold under which most firms do not export, owing to the fixed costs of exporting. The fixed costs result from more stringent quality controls, additional administration, transportation and marketing expenses, and the need to conform with the formal steps required for exporting.

Most firms export directly without going through traders. This was seen in the case of printing companies, since the highly precise product specifications require a close coordination between the firm and the client. Nevertheless, the absence of traders is more surprising in the other industries. One explanation is that executives of export firms believe that traders eat up the profit margins. If traders cannot cut their take, products become too expensive for export markets because Colombian industries do not manufacture these goods at low enough prices. Therefore, once the initial links to export markets are established, traders can be bypassed. At the same time, traders have also moved their activity to regions where the cost of producing manufactured goods is much lower, such as in Asia.

All the companies sell the same products in the domestic and export markets. Trade liberalization has eliminated the market segmentation that allowed firms to sell completely different products in these two markets, sending the better quality products abroad. Now, in most companies different production lines for the two markets are not found.

Nevertheless, the product mix for export tends to be different from that aimed at the domestic market. Larger companies, which tend to have a greater variety of products, export a product mix that is more expensive than the one sold at home. This choice makes sense given the higher transportation costs for exports than for products made for the domestic market. For instance, brochures—a relatively lighter product than books—represent a higher proportion of printing companies' exports than their production for the domestic market. Similarly, the clothing firms export goods that are the same as the ones sold domestically, but they tend to have a higher proportion of higher range products. One of these companies, which sells expensive suits for men, manufactures all its products on the same production lines, but uses expensive imported fabrics for export products.

The smaller companies export without a section set up exclusively for that purpose, and export negotiations are the responsibility of the firms' owners. As companies get larger, they start having nonexclusive agents abroad. The next step, as the size of the firm increases and/or exports grow, is to establish an export section. The largest firms have their own offices abroad. This progression results from a greater ability to cover administrative costs as the size of the firm increases. It also shows the need for agents closer to foreign clients as exports grow.

Learning by Exporting

Learning to export. Executives from a printing firm begin to export by going to trade fairs abroad. In a few cases, a company starts to export when a foreign client contacts it for that purpose. This first export experience often prompts the company's corporate managers to get more information about the export formalities and the available export assistance. In general, it is relatively easy for Colombian printing firms to export due to the printing industry's good reputation established by large companies such as Carvajal.

Leather products firms start exporting through business contacts made in the industry's trade fair in Bogotá. One of the industry's entrepreneurial associations asked Proexport, the Colombian TPO, to underwrite a trade fair in Bogotá instead of providing financing for companies to go to trade fairs abroad. The Bogotá trade fair has been very successful. A majority of the footwear and luggage firms included in the study started exporting through contacts made during these events. After a few initial export experiences company executives start going to trade fairs abroad, also with partial financial support from Proexport.

The interviews show that obtaining information about rules and regulations in faraway export markets can be difficult. For example, one of the food-processing companies had difficulties at first when finding out the requirements for U.S. Food and Drug Administration (FDA) approval. Provision of such information is important for firms that want to export.

In contrast, exporting to neighboring markets in Latin America does not require much information about standards, since they are quite similar. Sending goods to the regional markets, such as Venezuela or other countries of the Comunidad Andina, requires fewer efforts than exporting to other regions. For the regional markets, a key element that can be more difficult than gathering information is organizing the logistics to allow goods to reach their final destination. This is particularly important in the export of perishable goods.

Learning from exporting. The executives interviewed in the study said that exporting provides them with learning opportunities. A primary opportunity is in trade fairs, where products can be compared with the company's products and where main trends in an industry are established. The fairs also provide an occasion for finding out about new inputs and contacting suppliers. At the same time, a firm's executives can identify their main competitors and establish a sort of benchmarking.

The relationship with the clients from abroad also allows firms to get on a steeper learning curve. Some of the clients send consultants to assist the exporting firm, thereby allowing it to improve its production practices and to upgrade more rapidly—not to mention establishing links with an updated consultant network.

For example, one of the manufacturers interviewed in Bogotá became a supplier of men's leather footwear for JCPenney and Wal-Mart. In that process, the U.S. companies provided the standards required for the products' acceptability. This made the firms' technicians pay attention to many details of which they had been unaware. As a result, the company was able not only to be a successful exporter, but also improve the quality of its products for other clients, domestic as well as foreign.

Several of the other corporate managers have had similar experiences. Exporting allows them to learn better production practices so as to comply with international standards; this in turn enables them to increase their market share in the domestic market.

Exporting is particularly useful for learning about quality standards and quality control practices, since export markets are often more demanding. The executives interviewed also believe that selling abroad has enabled them to streamline their companies to better meet deadlines.

One of the few company executives who said that exporting has not provided him with learning opportunities attributed this to the fact that he began making footwear *after* visiting the plants of leading manufacturers in the United States, such as Timberland. He has also hired an American consultant to assist him in setting up the firm.

The manager of one of the footwear trade associations believes that the export firms in his industry are those that are in the best position to protect themselves from competing imports due to lessons learned in international markets.

However, there is a difference between the learning process observed in Colombian firms and that in the Chilean and the Mexican companies in the project. Chilean firms (and even more so Mexican ones) rapidly introduce the changes in all their production lines, but the same is not true for all Colombian firms. For example, one Colombian food-processing firm manufactures candies for the United States following FDA standards, while it continues selling candies with FDA-forbidden additives in Colombia and other Latin American countries.

Colombian firm executives often have an attitude different from that observed in the other two countries, particularly Mexico. The corporate managers of exporting Mexican manufacturing firms see their domestic market and the U.S. market as one single market. In this sense, the learning process from exporting is not as strong in Colombia as it is in Chile and Mexico.

The main explanations for the lower intensity of the export learning process in Colombian firms in contrast to that in Chilean and Mexican ones are the following. First, learning is stimulated by competition and exposure to demanding international standards. Import competition in Colombia is less intense than in the other two countries.

Second, Colombian entrepreneurs, who are among the most dynamic entrepreneurs interviewed during the investigation, spend a considerable amount of time and energy trying to overcome the numerous obstacles they face when trying to manufacture and export. Therefore, they have less time and energy to focus on exploiting all the potential learning opportunities derived from exporting.

Third, learning to manufacture goods that can compete in world markets requires that companies have easy and expeditious access to imported inputs. This condition is not always fulfilled in Colombia.

Export Promotion Policies: Usefulness for Export Firms

One of the goals of the research was to evaluate the export promotion instruments from the perspective of firms. Companies' executives were asked if they benefited from policy instruments when exporting. This was done without mentioning the specific instruments so that the interview would reveal whether the instruments were known or not.

The interviews showed that Colombia has a quite efficient export promotion system when seen from the perspective of individual companies. Eighteen of the twenty-one firms included in the survey make use of the export promotion instruments, which was to be expected since the country is a pioneer in this field.

The export financing provided by the Banco de Comercio Exterior de Colombia (BANCOLDEX) is the most frequently used export promotion instrument. Companies often have difficulties in obtaining export credit from other financial institutions because borrowers have assets that cannot be seized in case of default. That credit is available is useful for export firms, and in fact Colombian companies have better access to export financing than those in most other Latin American countries.

In addition to its availability, the financing provided by BANCOLDEX has two advantages. First of all, the interest rates (though no longer subsidized) are generally lower than those offered on the domestic market. At the same time, the loans are available for longer periods than commercial bank loans.

The largest companies included in the study are not using BANCOLDEX's export financing as intensively as in the past because they can get comparable financing elsewhere. The smaller firms, which have difficulty in gaining access to financing in general—and to export financing in particular—do use the institution's loans frequently. In fact, one reason that a few of the firms included in the study began to export was precisely to get export financing.

For example, a visit to the plant of one of the Bogotá garment firms in the study revealed an impressive set of new, up-to-date equipment for dyeing fabric. The purchase of this equipment had been heavily subsidized by export financing, during the last period of intensive export subsidies, and having such equipment allowed the company a preferred-supplier certificate from Reebok. This in turn permitted the firm to attract other foreign buyers, thus contributing to an increase in exports.

The second most important export promotion instrument for the companies covered by the study was the Plan Vallejo. Most corporate managers said that it would be very difficult to export without the assistance provided by this scheme. However, this incentive is not compatible with the new rules of the Uruguay Round and will have to be modified.

CERT, the tax credit scheme, is the third most important export promotion instrument mentioned by the executives interviewed. However, corporate managers often complain about the reduction in the tax credit percentage and, above all, about the frequent changes in the amount to be credited. The fluctuations make it difficult for executives to estimate the returns they will get from exporting. In any event, this instrument must also be phased out in the coming years—for nonagricultural products—to allow the country to comply with its commitments in the Uruguay Round.

Firm executives interviewed believe that Proexport provides useful export assistance. The TPO's support for trade fair participation, both in organizing trade fairs in the country itself and in providing partial financing for participation in trade fairs abroad is very useful. Some of the firms included in the study were participating in the program of Unidades Exportadoras aimed at organizing export firms by industry.

While some of the executives interviewed stated that the assistance provided by Proexport's offices abroad was poor, most of those interviewed believe that it is useful. For instance, several executives avoid having to finance offices abroad by using Proexport's facilities.

Firm managers express a pervasive nostalgia for the period when Colombia had promotion instruments that allowed companies to benefit substantially from exporting. In those years, the 1970s and 1980s, export subsidies through tax credits were significant—and at the same time rates for export financing were subsidized.

Moreover, the fact that these export subsidy programs were not designed from the start as short-lived temporary support to firms in their initial export push made entrepreneurs believe that the programs should be permanent.

Advantages for and Obstacles to Exporting

Companies' exporting capability is strongly influenced by the advantages and obstacles they meet in their economic environment. This section will describe the main obstacles faced by Colombian firms when they export, as well as the chief advantages. Last, the obstacles that are most directly related to policy will be discussed.

A first obstacle faced by the firms included in the study is specific to their industry. Printing firm executives complain about the poor quality of the inputs available on the domestic market, but, at the same time, they have considerable difficulties in importing inputs due to problems in Colombia's customs. The difficulties in getting access to good-quality inputs restrain the companies' exports. In comparison, competing firms in other countries, such as Chilean printing firms, have easy, inexpensive, and prompt access to high-quality imported inputs.

The firms that use leather as an input also face serious problems because of the widespread violence in the Colombian countryside. Guerrilla, paramilitary, and drug dealer activities have led to a sharp decrease in cattle breeding. This has cut the domestic supply of leather. Meanwhile, the problems with customs make imported inputs very costly.

By contrast, one of the advantages accruing to the food-processing firms covered by the project is the availability of inexpensive and good-quality sugar in the domestic market. Likewise, printing firm executives believe that the excellent reputation of the Colombian printing industry is very helpful when they look for new clients abroad.

At the same time, other obstacles are not industry specific and are faced by a number of firms. First, the general climate of uncertainty pervasive in Colombia in recent years has had a negative impact on investment decisions. Second, the appreciation of the peso during the 1990s adversely affected the export performance of the firms in the survey.

Moreover, shipping to export markets is difficult due to the low frequency of shipments and high cost, both caused in part by a poor transportation infrastructure. There are yet the difficulties for importing, which may become less relevant if the barriers to legal imports are reduced.

Another obstacle is smuggling, which is estimated to be as high as 1% of GDP (DANE 1999a). Smuggling was supposed to decrease as the country cut tariffs and liberalized trade in the early 1990s, yet it has grown substantially.

The firms most directly hurt by smuggling are those with products that compete with the smuggled goods. The fact that the firms lose market share to smuggled goods weakens them in the domestic market and therefore impairs their ability to export. Even though smuggling does not introduce goods that compete with all those of the firms included in the project, it hurts all the companies. It is more costly for firms to work in the formal market; those companies that operate in the informal economy pay no taxes.

Inadequate infrastructure is a very significant obstacle for export firms: the poor state of ports, airport facilities, and roads, and the problems with energy supply, are extremely costly for companies. This is one barrier that corporate managers mention repeatedly. In fact, a visitor to the industrial neighborhoods can observe a striking contrast between the evident investment inside manufacturing plants and the deplorable state of the roads that lead to them. This is more so the case in Bogotá than in Medellín.

Of course, the worst obstacle to exporting is the general violence in the country. The first cost of the violence is the high expense of ensuring security both inside plants and when transporting goods and employees to and from production facilities. Medellín, for example, is still recovering from the war waged by the drug lord Pablo Escobar against extradition, which caused widespread bombings and killings in the city. There was evidence of the damage to infrastructure, as well as to lives during most of the interviews. Furthermore, the high probability of export shipments' being highjacked on their way to a port is pushing some companies to move their plants to coastal locations—or to neighboring countries.

Companies face substantial costs in certifying that drugs are not included in their shipments, to avoid ruining their reputation abroad. In line with the drug problem, Colombian firms also face higher costs than other companies in the region because Colombian firms' goods have to undergo thorough inspections when they get to the United States. Naturally, clients abroad are often reluctant to import from Colombia because of the risk of receiving shipments containing drugs (if this happens, the whole shipment could be seized by the authorities).

The climate of violence scares foreign clients away. They are often disinclined to visit the plants, even though the visits are generally required if a firm is to be certified as a supplier to large companies abroad. As well, corporate managers have difficulties in hiring consultants from abroad. One food-processing firm that deals in dairy products found it increasingly hard to convince Swiss consultants to assist in upgrading the quality of the products.

Nevertheless, executives interviewed believe that their firms also have advantages in their own environment. The first advantage, and one mentioned by every executive, is the country's location: Colombia is close to both the United States and Latin American markets. An entrepreneur from Medellín pointed out that his plant is four hours away by plane from the East Coast of the United States, closer than some firms in that very country, and the geographical proximity to Venezuela is also considered a strong advantage.

Good-quality human capital—both entrepreneurial capability and availability of skilled workers—is another advantage that corporate managers believe to be very important. Every executive interviewed in Medellín mentioned this, which is quite in contrast to other countries in Latin America where entrepreneurs often complain about their employees' low productivity.

Corporate managers believe that the system of efficient export promotion institutions is a major advantage. In fact, most firm executives feel that the only government institutions they have collaborative relationships with are precisely these TPOs.

Entrepreneurs also feel that the red tape involved in exporting is much greater than necessary. They believe that the frequent changes in export promotion policy (e.g., percentages applied to the CERT and changes in other export rules) make it very difficult to plan long-term investment in export activities. The same is true for the irregularity in the time taken by the government to give out tax credit certificates and refunds. A change in the delay of from 30 to 180 days can dramatically increase the financial cost for a firm.

Furthermore, in contrast to their positive impression of export promotion institutions, executives feel that the other government agencies do all they can to hinder productivity and export growth.

The most significant export barrier put up by the government is customs: getting inputs through customs is a painful ordeal that can take anywhere from two weeks to forty days. Some firms pay the cost of transporting their goods by air only to find that it takes the goods twenty days to clear customs. The practice of inspecting a high percentage of the shipments coming into the country is one cause for delay. The unpredictable delays, combined with theft from the goods in customs, and the frequent changes in the rules and requirements by custom officials, increase the cost of importing inputs. Thus companies have to carry higher inventories, which requires a larger amount of working capital.

For instance, the CEO of very large printing company in Bogotá explained that in the early 1990s it was possible to import a spare part that he needed urgently and then to complete the paperwork required to do so. At the time of the interviews, the paperwork had to be completed before the part was allowed into the country. This kind of red tape, combined with the delay in getting the part out of customs, forces him to keep several parts in stock and therefore increases his costs.

The difficulties in getting goods through customs are sometimes considered the result of lobbies pressuring the government to slow the import of competing goods. For instance, delays in importing fabric and the use of reference prices for customs valuation purposes for textile imports are widely attributed to pressure by textile manufacturers.

Entrepreneurs believe that the difficulties for importing are a significant source of cost increases. They also find the difficulties irritating in the extreme, considering that the country is flooded with smuggled goods. And, of course, the difficulty in getting goods through customs encourages smuggling.

The Influence of the Preferential Trade Agreements on Firms' Business Opportunities

Colombia's membership in the PTA with the Andean countries, the Comunidad Andina (formerly the Grupo Andino), has allowed the nation's companies to see the other countries of this customs union as an extension of the companies' domestic market. This is particularly so for Ecuador and Venezuela.

Half of the firms included in the study cited Venezuela as one of the main export markets. In effect, the trade agreement signed with that country in December 1991 has had the strongest influence on these companies' export opportunities.

The impact of the trade agreement among Colombia, Mexico, and Venezuela (the G-3) on business opportunities has not been significant because exports to Mexico plummeted after the 1994 Mexican peso devaluation. The interviews showed that Mexico had been an important market for the Colombian manufacturing firms before the devaluation, but that was due to some extent to the appreciation of the Mexican peso.

The entrepreneurs interviewed for the project found it easier to begin exporting to neighboring countries and then to move on to more demanding markets. Therefore, the regional PTAs provide an opportunity for firms to begin developing their export capability.

Conclusions

Colombia has had exemplary export promotion policies for decades. The policies it used to assist export firms were very effective over a long period given import substitution development strategy, needs of export companies, and former multilateral trade rules applicable to developing countries.

The state of affairs at the end of the 1990s is radically different. The country is no longer following an import substitution development strategy. The growing complexity of the challenges faced by firms in export markets implies the need to bring up to date the policies required for export assistance. Moreover, Colombia's commitments to the

Uruguay Round Agreements entail phasing out export subsidies for non-agricultural goods.

In these circumstances, the need remains for the country to have export promotion policies that allow it to increase and diversify nontraditional exports. This would enable it to become less vulnerable to the fluctuations in the price of oil and of coffee.

At the same time, a growing number of Colombian manufacturing firms need to export in order to have the scale and the technologies to maintain market share in the domestic market. Hence, the domestic and export markets complement each other by allowing companies to make better use of their installed capacity (for some companies) or to shift to a more efficient scale (for others). Moreover, the project's findings show that exporting provides firms with important learning opportunities and that these could be even greater if obstacles to importing and exporting were reduced. Effective export promotion policies would also allow companies to have a higher productivity and to get on steeper learning curves.

Up to now, the CERT and the SIEX/Plan Vallejo have been the instruments used by exporters to offset or to be exempted from the taxes paid when importing inputs used for exports. The CERT has the advantage that the payments are easy to calculate. The SIEX/Plan Vallejo is also relatively simple to use. However, the payments made to exporters under these schemes may have a subsidy component because the payments do not correspond strictly to the amount of taxes paid on imported inputs. Therefore, they will have to be modified to comply with Colombia's commitments with the Uruguay Round Agreements.

At the same time, the evidence discussed above shows that the CERT and the Plan Vallejo have outlived their effectiveness since they are no longer contributing to increasing and diversifying exports.

The transformation of the CERT and the SIEX/Plan Vallejo to comply with the new multilateral trade rules provides a good opportunity for Colombia to set up a new coherent export promotion strategy that will be functional for facing the challenges of exporting in the years ahead.

Colombia has already taken a step in the right direction by cutting tariffs, since these are the main source of an antiexport bias. The best way of encouraging exports is to decrease the antiexport bias instead of subsidizing exporters to offset it.

In addition to reducing this bias by cutting tariffs, exporting must be facilitated by policies that allow export firms to have access to competitively priced inputs and to avoid paying taxes twice, that is, both in Colombia and in the country exports go to.

First, Colombia must make sure that it has a streamlined drawback scheme that allows export firms to promptly obtain refunds for the duties paid when importing inputs to manufacture export goods. An efficient drawback system has not been important up to now, since firms could use the CERT and the Plan Vallejo. Nonetheless, it will become essential as these schemes are modified or phased out for non-agricultural exports.

Second, companies should also have access to a system that exempts them from paying duties on inputs imported to manufacture exports. The difference between this instrument and the drawback is that the first one allows export firms to suspend payment of taxes on imported inputs, whereas the drawback implies a refund. The drawback scheme is customarily used by occasional exporters. Companies that export continually prefer exemption from taxes on imported inputs because it decreases the need for working capital. If the goal is to encourage firms to export regularly, they should be able to use a duty exemption system that is efficient and easy to use. The Plan Vallejo for inputs presently in use is a good proxy for such a system, though care must be taken so that it is not taken for an export subsidy.

Both instruments are aimed at avoiding double taxation and at providing a free-trade regime. The instruments are not properly export promotion instruments, but they are key policy schemes for a country wanting to encourage nontraditional exports.

The formalities required to benefit from these instruments should be as simple as possible to keep red tape from being an export obstacle. Efficient drawback and duty exemption schemes that are streamlined, operate quickly, and are easily accessible to most firms provide the best foundation for policies seeking to facilitate exporting.

The time taken by government agencies to grant authorization to use export promotion schemes should be limited to a few weeks. There should be an understanding that if no additional information is requested and no objection is presented within a short time—say two weeks—the authorization for using the instrument will be automatically granted. The public sector's experience in managing such schemes as the Plan Vallejo and the CERT indicates that the sector should be able to acquire the ability to administer the new instruments.

It is important that the government make efforts to set up the new instruments as soon as possible. The data available on exports using the

CERT, the SIEX/Plan Vallejo, and the interviews with corporate managers demonstrate that exporters are heavily dependent on these two schemes. This implies that the instruments replacing them should be in place as soon as possible.

One possible option is to initially establish the duty exemption system for firms that have a long-standing export record and then progressively extend it to other firms. A good example is the ALTEX Program in Mexico.

The study of successful export firms demonstrates that the export financing provided by BANCOLDEX has a significant impact on the firms. In fact, export financing is the export promotion instrument most frequently used by the firms included in the research. Concurrently, Proexport is very effective in assisting export firms by providing information and support for trade fair participation and by creating strategies to export specific goods through the Unidades Exportadoras. Exporters can also use the agency's offices abroad as a base during their business trips.

Nevertheless, the present structure of Proexport and BANCOLDEX must be assessed to make sure that these institutions have the potential to provide export firms with the support needed to export nontraditional goods in the years ahead. This is indispensable because the assistance provided to exporters by these two institutions will become decisive as the subsidies provided through the CERT and the SIEX/Plan Vallejo are eliminated. Therefore, it is important to ensure that these TPOs are as effective as possible in encouraging new firms to export and that more occasional exporters have a permanent presence in markets abroad. The recent measures aimed at ensuring that credit from BANCOLDEX is available to small and medium-sized exporters are a step in the right direction. The same can be said of the current changes in Proexport's structure that demonstrate the government's determination to improve that TPO's performance.

Instituting efficient drawback and duty exemption schemes and ensuring that Proexport and BANCOLDEX are as effective as is possible should be the main goals of a new export promotion strategy for Colombia, one that will allow it to increase nontraditional exports. Only when these tasks are accomplished should the government start considering other policies that have the potential of contributing to exporting new goods while being WTO compatible. At the same time, it would be useful to lay out new measures aimed at facilitating exporting services. Most of the export promotion instruments used by Colombia—and by the other Latin American countries—are not appropriate for encouraging the export of services.

Once the government—working closely with the private sector—has established what the new foundations of the export promotion strategy are to be, it should ensure that the policies are stable and that they do not constantly vary.

Entrepreneurs, whether or not they export, need a long-term horizon in which to plan their investments. One of the most frequent complaints expressed by corporate managers during the interviews was that the frequent changes in export promotion policies (such as the percentage of tax rebate granted through the CERT) made it very difficult to make investment decisions. As a result, entrepreneurs are often reluctant to invest important amounts in export projects, given that the rules change recurrently.

The government should make sure that the instruments described above are not revised to counter short-run fiscal contingencies. Such schemes as the drawback and duty exemption are not incentives, but strictly policies to avoid having exports pay taxes twice, in Colombia and the importing country.

In addition to policies that assist export firms, the government should try to decrease export obstacles as much as possible. Not even the most efficient export promotion system in the world nor the best negotiated PTA can compensate companies for the antiexport bias that results from the numerous obstacles they face when trying to export.

The main export obstacle in Colombia, the persistent state of violence, is outside the powers of the authorities in charge of trade policies and thus beyond the reach of this chapter. But another important barrier to export—the poor state of the infrastructure—is partly due to the violence, which will take a long time to reduce. There are, however, other obstacles that can be eliminated more easily and that are within the capabilities of the Ministerio de Comercio Exterior, the ministry responsible for trade.

The chief obstacle to export within the reach of the trade ministry is customs, which should stop being mainly a tax-collecting entity and a barrier to imports competing with domestic goods. Many entrepreneurs believe that the practice customs has of inspecting a high proportion of import shipments—thus substantially increasing the delay for clearing goods—is in fact the result of protectionist pressures applied by domestic industrial lobbies. Whether this is true of not, it would be much more efficient to carry out random checks and set high penalties for infractions. Entrepreneurs also find that the cumbersome customs procedures are particularly galling in light of widespread smuggling.

The Pastrana administration's export program shows that increasing exports, particularly nontraditional exports with higher value added, has a high priority. Several of the measures adopted recently (e.g., getting exports through customs, slashing the red tape for export formalities, and cutting smuggling) clearly confirm this priority and the administration's determination to move ahead in this. At the same time, phasing out the CERT for nonagricultural products and limiting the use of the Plan Vallejo exclusively for inputs demonstrates the government's willingness to comply with the Uruguay Round Agreements. The export program set forth by the present administration could have an important positive impact on export growth if the measures it suggests are all carried out and if other policy aspects that are key to export growth are also guided in the proper direction. One of these is the behavior of the exchange rate.

Exchange rate appreciation is an issue that is beyond the reach of the Ministry of Foreign Trade. Yet, peso appreciation has an important impact on export performance, both in the short term through its influence on the ability of Colombian exporters to compete with goods from other countries (in the domestic market and abroad) and in the long term, since it provides a disincentive for investing in export projects.

A certain degree of appreciation is to be expected if the country is a successful exporter and productivity increases. Nevertheless, the extent of the sustained appreciation of the Colombian peso since the early 1990s damaged exporting. (The depreciation during 1998 has somewhat offset this problem.) Yet it must be stressed that it is preferable, from the standpoint of promoting exports, to avoid a substantial appreciation and at the same time to avoid sharp devaluations. The optimal policy is to aim for a currency that is stable over the long run and that appreciates chiefly in proportion to improvements in productivity.

Colombia was a pioneer in export promotion policies in Latin America for many decades. The new state of affairs—a new development strategy, the more complex challenges faced by export companies, and the multilateral trade rules arising from the Uruguay Round Agreements—has compelled the country's government to design a new strategy for increasing nontraditional exports. Colombia is once again becoming a forerunner in designing the new policies that are appropriate for promoting exports in light of the challenges faced by firms in the years ahead. From that perspective, the strategy set forth in Colombia's new export plan is a good example for the Latin American governments that want to promote higher export growth rates that are sustainable in the long run.

Notes

1. I would like to acknowledge the contribution of Ms. Magdalena Pardo for the study on the behavior of export firms and in preparing a background paper that was used for writing this chapter (Pardo 1996). She is not responsible for the views expressed in this chapter. The information provided by Colombia's Ministerio de Comercio Exterior is also gratefully acknowledged.

2. All the information in this section, unless otherwise specified, is from ECLAC (1999b) and (1999c).

3. Information provided by Colombia's Ministry of Foreign Trade.

4. This section does not describe free-trade zones, since they were not included in the research. The first law allowing free-trade zones in Colombia is from 1958, but the reforms of 1991 also authorized private entrepreneurs to set up such zones. Several privately managed free-trade zones have been set up in Bogotá, Cali, Cartagena, and Medellín since then.

5. Therefore, customs has given the highest priority to collecting taxes. This has had negative implications for the productive sector (Pardo 1996).

6. Information provided by the Ministry of Foreign Trade.

7. Information provided by the Ministry of Foreign Trade.

8. Exports to Bolivia, Ecuador, and Venezuela—members of the Comunidad Andina—have been excluded from using the CERT since 1993. Exports to Peru can still benefit from this instrument (Garay et al. 1998).

9. Presentation made by Mr. Diaz Uribe, Director of Proexport's Representation in Chile during the World Conference of Trade Promotion Organizations, Santiago, October 1998.

10. Information provided by the Ministry of Trade.

11. See Carla Macario (1998d) for a detailed description of the firms included in the study, the criteria for selecting them, and the main findings of the research.

12. Industries that are successful exporters mainly due to an intrinsic natural-resource comparative advantage were excluded from the study. The same criterion was used for the research in the other countries.

6

Conclusions and Recommendations: Policies for Export Growth

Carla Macario

Latin American and Caribbean countries have achieved significant transformations in their macroeconomic and trade policies during the past decade. They have set aside import substitution strategies and have opened up their economies. The new economic model has given a high priority to increasing exports.

Yet Latin America's export performance is still deficient. The region's share of world exports has decreased from 5.8% in 1983 to 5.3% in 1997 (WTO 1998a). This demonstrates that the countries in the region are not taking advantage of the considerable opportunities resulting from the expansion of global trade. At the same time, most of the countries' economies depend on a few export products (ECLAC 1999a). Moreover, the bulk of exports are still commodities, which are highly sensitive to international market fluctuations. Furthermore, commodities have the additional disadvantage of prices that tend to decline relative to the prices of manufactured goods and that will continue to do so during the coming decades (World Bank 1999).

Latin American exports of manufactured goods are for the most part countercyclical, so that they fall when demand recovers in the domestic markets. The only exceptions, to a certain extent, are Barbados and Brazil. The other exception is Mexico, which has managed to have a spectacular growth of its manufactured exports (see Chapters 1 and 2). The majority of the other countries in the region still lacks the capability to sustain continuous exports of high-value-added goods.

However, the export promotion instruments presently used by the governments in the region are for the most part insufficient for acquiring this capability. Most Latin American countries, therefore, will have to redraft their export promotion policies to ensure that they are effective in light of the challenges now faced by export firms.

The future export promotion strategies will need to be fully compatible with the Uruguay Round Agreements by the year 2003. The new rules that result from these agreements will have important consequences for developing countries. To begin with, the rules open the way for improved market access and permit a strengthened dispute settlement procedure, thus favoring smaller nations. Moreover, the rules will entail significant affects on the export policy environment, because several of the instruments customarily used in free-trade zones need to be modified or eliminated.

The most important multilateral rules regarding export promotion polices are set forth in the Agreement on Subsidies and Countervailing Measures of the Final Act of the Uruguay Round signed at Marrakesh (GATT 1994). This agreement defines subsidies and limits the possibility that countries have of using export subsidies for nonagricultural goods. Subsidies contingent on export performance or on the use of domestic goods over imported ones are prohibited. At the same time, it allows subsidies for industrial research and precompetitive development activity, assistance to disadvantaged regions, and support for companies' adaptation to new environmental requirements, provided that the assistance for environmental requirements meet a set of specifications. Developing countries are granted a special and differential treatment in that the agreement does not apply to the poorest developing nations and that the other developing-country members have a longer period in which to comply with its provisions.

Therefore, nonagricultural export subsidies will have to be cut in the vast majority of Latin American and Caribbean nations. Even in those countries (that are among the least developed nations) that can subsidize nonagricultural exports without breaking the WTO rules, it would make no sense to allocate large sums for this purpose. The new rules on nonagricultural export subsidies, far from hindering export development in the long run, will put greater pressure on governments to address inefficiencies at the source and to focus resources on increasing productivity in the entire economy. This is the best way of developing a sustainable export capability. Hence, the key issue that must be addressed is what export promotion policies are relevant under the present circumstances (Tussie and Lengyel 1998).

Nevertheless, in the region there is a wide disparity about the need to renovate these policies. There are some countries that will have to rebuild the foundations of their export promotion strategies, while some others already have instruments that are effective and fully compatible with the WTO requirements and therefore require only minor adjustments to reach a larger number of firms.

This chapter lays out a wide range of policy recommendations that need to be adapted to the specific needs of a given country after establishing the government's priorities.

It must be pointed out that the proposals in this chapter involve decisions by numerous high-ranking civil servants, not only those in charge of the TPOs. Nevertheless, it is necessary to stress that it is important that managers in charge of TPOs realize that they must attempt to ensure the application of these proposals even when the proposals are beyond their immediate responsibilities. TPO executives should discard the notion of simply focusing on export promotion instruments while setting aside the other issues mentioned here. For instance, promoting exports without facilitating imports is a mercantilist notion that will be fruitless for developing a sustainable export capability. TPO managers will be most successful if they view themselves as trade facilitators and assume the responsibility of promoting trade, facilitating imports as well as exports, and trying to remove obstacles to trade. If these managers fail to do so, their efforts to promote exports will have few chances of being successful. Trade should be facilitated in general if export activity is to be encouraged.

Arguments for Policies to Promote Exports

Do Latin American countries really need export promotion policies? This is the first issue that must be addressed. In fact, if there are no compelling arguments to justify instruments that encourage firms to export it would be wrong to allocate resources for such a purpose. In fact, it would then be preferable not to have export promotion policies at all, thus contributing to streamlining policy and to allowing the use of government funds for programs that have higher priorities. Therefore, this section presents reasons for which countries should contemplate export promotion policies.

First, such policies are needed to compensate for the antiexport bias. This bias has been considerably reduced in the Latin American and Caribbean countries during the recent years, but it still is prevalent in many nations. The first source of the antiexport bias is the presence of tariffs. Even if tariffs have been cut and are low in comparison with those of the past decades, they are still often relatively high. Nontariff barriers have also been cut but are still pervasive. On top of these, firms that want to export often face many obstacles that lead to concentrating on domestic markets. This is all compounded by weak competition policies, which also contribute to making manufacturing for the domestic market more profitable than exporting. If the goal is to make it as profitable to invest in exporting goods with high value added as it is to invest in manufacturing for the domestic market or in a limited range of natural-resource-intensive commodities, there is a need for policies that encourage companies to become exporters.

Second, there are positive externalities arising from the export activity of pioneer export companies. These positive externalities benefit other firms in the country. Pioneer export companies often have to spend a significant amount of time and financial resources to be able to begin exporting. Yet, once they have managed to break into foreign markets, their export success immediately provides a signal to other firms in the same industry. Other companies often begin to export a given product following the example of a leading firm. Pioneer export firms face higher costs than latecomer companies because the pioneers have to make attempts in several markets before being successful. (They also face the risk of failing.) In contrast, the followers in an export market incur lower costs. Hence, the investment in new export industries will be suboptimal if the assistance for firms exporting new products or to new markets is inadequate.

Third, exporting allows firms access to economies of scale. This is particularly the case for companies based in medium and small-sized economies. From a theoretical perspective, the introduction of economies of scale in the trade models has substantially improved the consistency of the predictions of these models with the stylized facts that characterize trade nowadays (see Chapter 1). At the same time, economies of scale are among the chief sources of the increase of trade of nontraditional goods following the PTAs signed by Latin American countries in past years (Devlin and Ffrench-Davis 1999).

Providing companies with assistance that enables them to start exporting increases their efficiency by fostering a shift of their production function toward a larger scale. It also allows firms to acquire updated technologies. This, in turn, leads to productivity improvements and strengthens the companies' positions in the face of import competition in the domestic market. Consequently, Latin American firms should be encouraged to sell on export markets in addition to their domestic market business. The export and the domestic markets should be viewed as complementary. Being a successful exporter allows a company to offset the fluctuations of demand in the domestic market, but at the same time a strong standing in the domestic market enables a company to cover the costs incurred when it breaks into markets abroad.

Fourth, exporting allows firms to get on steeper learning curves than when they sell only in the domestic market. Companies are forced to develop the ability to face the intense competition on export markets and the more stringent standards of their foreign clients. Simultaneously, companies have access to better information that allows them to accelerate upgrading.

To manufacture higher quality products, companies have to upgrade equipment operating on the production line and improve quality control practices. At the same time, closer contact with more sophisticated clients enables export firm managers to closely follow the trends and innovations in their specific market. This allows them to introduce new products. In other words, exporting forces companies to modernize their production and distribution practices.

This accelerated learning by exporting is not restricted to the firm that sells the product abroad. The ability to manufacture higher quality products is partly dependent on upgrading inputs. Therefore, the pressure to upgrade also reaches the domestic suppliers to these exporting companies, because the domestic suppliers' products have to progressively meet higher standards. The upgrading of the export products and the domestic inputs used to make them has positive spillovers in the domestic market as improved production practices disseminate throughout the economy. Consequently, providing assistance for firms that are beginning to export is a way of fostering a faster learning process and increasing productivity.

Measures to Decrease the Antiexport Bias

The first step that must be taken to decrease the antiexport bias is to target one of its main sources, that is to cut tariff rates as much as possible within a range that is consistent with the other priorities of economic policy. Reducing tariffs is essential, since a significant part of their cost is ultimately borne by exports (Clements and Sjaastad 1984). The tariff schedule must be assessed by comparing it with those that prevail in other nations at the time and by estimating which tariff rates would lead to a greater increase in productivity and exports. By contrast, using the past history of tariffs as the main reference is not advisable. Next, measures should be taken to reduce nontariff barriers, which have become more binding as tariffs have been cut in Latin American countries.

At the same time, governments should take steps to reduce or eliminate as much as possible the inefficiencies that pose obstacles to export firms (Laird 1999). The main principle that should guide this action is to address the source of inefficiencies instead of paying out subsidies to offset their consequences. The experience in most Latin American countries during the past decades shows that export subsidies may have undesirable effects because they are often regressive and tend to concentrate on a small number of firms, some of which are large companies, both domestic and transnational.

Moreover, entrepreneurs often end up believing that subsidization should be permanent and are therefore not encouraged to upgrade and attain the productivity levels that would allow them to survive without such compensation. Furthermore, export subsidies can end up being very costly for the public sector's budget. From that perspective, the Uruguay Round Agreements have made a positive contribution by making it easier for governments to resist pressures from industrial lobbies that have thrived on these subsidies in the past.

Infrastructure deficiencies, for example, have traditionally been a significant export obstacle that critically impairs the export capability of companies. Port facilities that operate poorly, deficiencies in the provision of energy, inadequate telecommunication networks, and customs officials who delay shipments are some of the examples that persist in the region. The aggregate impact of these difficulties, the *costo país*, has up to now been partially offset with export subsidies.

The following recommendations are within the realm of the authorities responsible for trade policy. The recommendations seek to decrease the antiexport bias; but it must be pointed out that some of the measures suggested here may seem too rudimentary for Latin American countries that have updated their trade policy. They may also appear to reiterate Rhee's seminal work in this field (Rhee 1985).

Nevertheless, there are many nations in the region that have yet to complete their reforms in this matter. There are countries that still have tariffs that are high and that vary widely for different items, significant nontariff barriers, costly export subsidies, and drawback systems that in fact are inoperative. At the same time, there are other countries that are very advanced in this area and that have policies that are highly effective for promoting exports, while being fully compatible with the rules that are to be enforced by the WTO following the Uruguay Round Agreements.

Streamlining Formalities

One of the steps that should be carried out by a government beginning to overhaul the country's export promotion system is to make a detailed list of all the formalities that are required from exporters. This would enable the authorities to establish which formalities make sense at the present time and to discard all the others.

This recommendation may seem too simple for a person not closely associated with export activities. It certainly is too basic for those countries that have already made considerable efforts to upgrade export assistance. Nevertheless, there are many nations that still demand that exporters conform to too many regulations. These regulations discourage exporters, particularly those attempting to export for the first time. Moreover, many of these formalities were originally set up to deal with short-term contingencies during the import substitution period and have remained in place since then.

An example of this sort of obstacle to exporting is the requirement for export permits from such ministries as agriculture, health, or defense. In some cases, these formalities were initially established to restrict export of basic goods that were heavily subsidized with the goal of enhancing the welfare of consumers in the domestic market. So, it made perfect sense to control these goods' export. In most cases, these subsidies had already been phased out, but these regulations are still often required because of inertia and resistance by civil servants, who try to preserve as much discretionary power as they can.

Some Caribbean countries, for instance, require a specific sanitary permit and an authorization by their ministries of defense for every single export shipment. Exporting can require up to ten different steps—again for each shipment—while each of these steps involves going to offices in different locations and submitting copies of the forms already presented in another office. More recently, the bureaucracy associated with establishing the origin of a product to enable it to benefit from a PTA has become a stumbling block for exporters in those countries where the certificates are issued by a limited number of offices located exclusively in the capital.

If a government wishes to facilitate exporting, it should examine carefully all the export-related red tape and retain only the regulations that are justified under present circumstances. At the same time, care should be taken to ensure that the regulations retained are simple and expeditious. These streamlining decisions have no financial cost whatsoever; they simply require the political will to overcome the resistance of the bureaucracies in charge of the regulations. Costa Rica, for example, has carried out important reforms in this area and has been able to decrease the number of export formalities thanks to the efforts of the country's TPO, the Promotora de Comercio Exterior de Costa Rica (Monge 1998).

Another measure is to bring together in one place all the agencies that deal with export formalities by setting up a one-stop facility. This does not imply clumping together all the different organizations that are involved, such as ministries of commerce or finance or the agency in charge of managing customs. It simply means bringing together small offices of these agencies in one building to ensure that all the formalities can be carried out at the same time. That way, the exporter will not have to face a complicated and lengthy routine to complete the official paperwork. At the same time, gathering into one place the different agencies in charge of export formalities contributes to improving communication among the different government organizations and can also lead to further cutting export red tape.

The general guidelines that should be taken into account when streamlining export formalities are as follows:

- Export formalities should be *simplified* as much as possible.
- Required information should be easy to obtain and *transparent*.
- Export formalities should be completed *promptly*, and a maximum delay (e.g., two weeks) for dealing with the formalities must be established from the beginning.
- *Automatic* approval should be preferred to discretionary approval whenever possible, particularly for export firms that have established a reputation of complying with the requirements.
- All the steps should be carried out in a *one-stop facility*.
- And once all the formalities have been streamlined, the fundamental instruments should remain stable so as to minimize information costs.

Instruments to Allow Access to Competitive Inputs

An export company must have access to inputs at competitive prices and quality irrespective of whether they are imported or manufactured domestically. If this condition is not met, the company will be at a disadvantage with respect to its competitors in other countries.

Drawbacks. A drawback system that allows exporters to receive a rebate on duties paid on inputs imported for manufacturing exports is a requisite for enabling export companies to have access to competitive inputs. Contrary to what is often stated, this instrument is not an export promotion instrument that favors exporters above firms manufacturing for the domestic market. It is strictly a modality to prevent exporters from having to pay taxes twice, in both the importing and the exporting countries. Therefore, it is fully compatible with the Uruguay Round Agreements on export subsidies. Moreover, it is a way of decreasing the antiexport bias.

While some countries in Latin America have, in theory, a duty drawback mechanism, companies use them rarely because the drawbacks tend to require complex procedures and because it is more practical to apply for export subsidies. Nevertheless, this instrument should become more important in the coming years as nonagricultural export subsidies are phased out to comply with WTO rules.

This mechanism must operate simply and promptly, with a minimum of red tape. The requirements to be met in order to benefit from this policy instrument must be transparent and permanently established. At the same time, the government should be firmly committed to avoiding trying to solve short-term public-sector budget problems (as has often been the case in the past) by diverting the resources originally allocated for the drawback. Care must be taken to ensure that this instrument is indisputably a rebate on tariffs and not an export subsidy. This is indispensable in guaranteeing compatibility with the Uruguay Round Agreements on export subsidies for nonagricultural products. It must be pointed out that these agreements have widened the range of imported inputs that can qualify for duty drawback by allowing the inclusion of the imported inputs that are consumed in the production of the export product, such as fuel.

To go further, once the drawback system is working efficiently, governments must set up mechanisms that allow duty rebates for indirect exporters. This would allow domestic companies that supply inputs to export companies to get a rebate for the duties paid when importing goods. This kind of instrument, which has already been put in practice by Mexico, is essential for strengthening the backward linkages of exporting and for increasing the effect of export growth on the rest of the economy.[1]

Duty exemptions. While it is true that an efficient duty drawback system is essential—since it allows companies that export occasionally to avoid double taxation—firms that export on a regular basis need to be exempted from paying duties for inputs used to manufacture exports.[2] This instrument is essential for increasing the number of companies that export regularly.

A duty exemption scheme allows export firms to decrease the funds needed for working capital in comparison with those funds needed when using the drawback. Therefore, it is particularly important for small and medium-sized businesses. The advantages of an instrument that allows duty exemption instead of refund of duties, as in a drawback, are particularly relevant in countries that have high inflation rates or during periods of uncertainty over the exchange rate. In fact, effective duty exemption systems have strongly contributed to export growth in Mexico and in Asia (Rhee 1985).

Access to this program should be as automatic as possible while efforts are made to minimize discretionary decisions and uncertainty. The companies that have established a good exporting record should be able to fulfill the requirements swiftly. When the different duty exemption mechanisms presently in operation in Latin America are compared, the benefits of the system used by Mexico—which requires less paperwork than in other countries—are clear in that a larger proportion of firms make use of it. The most efficient method for managing this kind of instrument is to streamline regulations and procedures as much as possible when the applications are turned in and to set very high penalties for infractions discovered through random verification checks.

Duty exemption is compatible with the WTO rules, since it is aimed at avoiding double taxation and is not an export subsidy. Nevertheless, setting this system up requires that a government have a strong administrative competence: this prevents companies from using this exemption to avoid duties on inputs for manufacturing goods for the domestic market.

Export Promotion Policies

Many TPOs in Latin America have at some time or another provided assistance in increasing nontraditional exports. Nevertheless, they have not always been very effective in supporting export companies partly because of inadequate funding, administrative inefficiencies, and lack of a clear vision of what the chief mandate was.

Consequently, several countries in the region are overhauling their TPOs to make them more effective for increasing nontraditional exports. The need to ensure compatibility with the Uruguay Round Agreements has also played a role in the renewal of export promotion agencies. The most appropriate institutional structure for specific TPOs will ultimately depend on a country's priorities and can be decided with the technical cooperation of the international multilateral organizations that work in this field, such as the International Trade Centre UNCTAD/WTO.

It is important to point out that export promotion activities need not be restricted to the public sector. On the contrary, many of them could be the responsibility of private-sector institutions. As a matter of fact, there is a trend toward growing participation by the private sector in export promotion activities as firms or entrepreneurial associations carry out tasks that were formerly the exclusive responsibility of public-sector agencies. This course should be strongly encouraged, since it will enable export assistance to be more effective if there is proper supervision. Moreover, it promotes the establishment of close links between TPOs and the private sector, which are essential for the success of an export promotion strategy. At the same time, a process of competitive bidding for some of the funds allocated to export promotion may allow a more efficient use of the public funds earmarked for this purpose.

In addition to the growing provision of export services by private firms, there has been a change in the procedures of TPOs themselves, since they are following practices closer to those of the private sector. Some export agencies, for example, have started charging for their services and require cost sharing from the private firms, one of the motivations for this being inadequate funding and the need for access to better financing. Nevertheless, it also indicates what service firms are willing to pay for and allows a more efficient use of public funds. Moreover, it has the benefit of exposing TPOs to competition from private firms (Esser et al. 1995). Besides, it has led—in some cases—to activities being taken over by private firms as evidence is provided that there is demand for a specific service. The organization of trade fairs is one of the areas where this trend has become important.

At the same time, there is an expanding participation by the private sector in design of export promotion strategies and in management of TPOs. For instance, a board that has a majority of private-sector representatives manages Costa Rica's agency, PROCOMER (Alonso 1998). Similarly, the government of Chile has drafted a law, yet to be approved by Congress, which will increase the participation of the private sector in the management of ProChile, the country's TPO. In any event, the export assistance activities described below could be carried out both by public-sector TPOs, by competent private firms, or entrepreneurial associations.

Information

The first step an entrepreneur must take when trying to begin exporting is the gathering of information, which includes knowledge of the formalities required to export and the available export assistance programs. Next, guidance is needed concerning potential export markets, and tariff and nontariff barriers in those countries. Guidelines are needed with respect to such product characteristics in the specific markets as prices, quality requirements, and distribution networks. Moreover, exporters need to find out what the established practices are in a given market to pay for export shipments. This information needs to be periodically updated so that it reflects the changes that result, for example, from recent PTAs.

Obtaining this kind of information can be very costly in terms of time and financial resources for a company that is beginning to export. If entrepreneurs have difficulties in obtaining the information needed to export, they may be discouraged even before their first attempt. Moreover, the scarcity of information about export markets is regressive because it has a stronger impact on small and medium-sized firms. (Large companies will find it much easier to obtain the knowledge needed to export.)

An indication of the importance of information on export markets is that the countries in Latin America that supply effective assistance in this field are also those that are most successful in increasing the number of export companies. Mexico, for example, has given a high priority to providing information on export markets through the foreign trade bank, BANCOMEXT, and through the Secretaría de Comercio y Fomento Industrial, the ministry in charge of trade. At the same time, Chile provides information for export firms through ProChile and through the Asociación de Exportadores de Manufacturas, the entrepreneurial association that organizes companies exporting manufactured goods. Colombian firms have access to information through Proexport, the institution in charge of export promotion.

In contrast, the majority of the nations in the region provide very poor information services to export firms. This is true for the TPOs and also for the entrepreneurial associations that attempt to assist in this field. In such countries, individual firms have to make considerable efforts to gather the information they need to begin exporting.

Gathering the information needed to export can be very costly for individual companies. Supplying information on export markets is clearly a case of provision of a public good because the use of information by one firm does not prevent its use by another company. Moreover, pioneer export firms promptly provide a signal to other companies about which export markets can lead to greater chances of success. This implies that the provision of the information needed to sell abroad yields important positive externalities, and that the lack of information in this matter may result in a suboptimal investment in exporting. Therefore, assistance in this domain is critical irrespective of the agency that provides this support; it can be a governmental TPO or a private-sector institution (e.g., a company that specializes in disseminating information or an entrepreneurial association). Whatever the preferred institutional arrangement is, if the goal is to increase exports, the provision of the information needed to export is a requisite for increasing the number of export firms.

Assistance for Trade Fair Participation and Marketing Abroad

Participating in trade fairs is highly beneficial for entrepreneurs breaking into export markets. Participation provides advantages that go beyond getting immediate contracts for the company. Trade fairs provide a unique opportunity to learn the products being demanded, the best practices used by the industry, the range of inputs available, and the access to consultant networks and many other benefits available even for companies that did not have a display at the fair.

Trade promotion agencies have often provided companies with assistance to attend fairs. Nonetheless, this support can be fruitless when the specific trade fair is not adequate for the entrepreneurs receiving assistance. For instance, there are many trade fairs for the clothing industry. Some of these fairs deal exclusively with large shipments for department stores in the United States, and so they are often of no use for a great number of Latin American firms that can only manufacture small lots. It is important that both entrepreneurs and TPO officials consult with industry experts about the usefulness of going to any fair. This ensures that an entrepreneur benefits from going to an event and does not end up discouraged, and guarantees a useful allocation of the public funds assigned for this purpose.

Some countries have tried to maximize the contacts between domestic and foreign firms by organizing trade fairs at home and bringing buyers from abroad to a large-scale presentation of an industry's output. Colombia, for example, has done this: Proexport has financed the organization of trade fairs for the footwear industry in Bogotá and the travel expenses of foreign buyers. The outcome of these events has been very positive because many entrepreneurs have gotten their first export contract in these circumstances.

Another option is to organize trips for groups of executives in the same industry to trade fairs abroad. This allows enhancing the benefits of trade fair participation by stimulating communication among the entrepreneurs. Chile and Colombia have done this for several years with very good results. Moreover, these trips can be combined with technological excursions, that is with visits to plants that have scales and technologies that may be useful as benchmarks for the entrepreneurs (Ramos 1997).

Companies that attempt to break into export markets have to develop the capability of marketing abroad. Assistance by a TPO can be essential in this area. Yet, the importance of marketing abroad can vary widely from one industry to another. Marketing abroad and looking for new clients is less important for firms that manufacture commodities than for companies that manufacture differentiated goods. Companies exporting commodities usually have a stable and relatively small group of clients. By contrast, firms exporting, for example, specific food products need to be in permanent contact with the market to keep up with the rapidly changing tastes.

These differences between industries are relevant for marketing abroad. The support needed by these different kinds of companies is not the same, and civil servants working in TPOs need to be aware of this. The export promotion activities have to be closely in tune with the needs of the specific industries receiving assistance.

Export Financing and Insurance

Export financing is an important component of an export promotion strategy. Export companies should be able to provide their clients with financing terms that are similar to the ones offered by their competitors from other countries. If the companies are unable to do so, they have less chance of obtaining export orders. In fact, firms from some Latin American nations often fail to obtain export contracts due to their inability to provide clients with financing. This is particularly true for some industries that offer equipment in which long-term financing is a standard practice.

The Uruguay Round Agreements accept export credit and export insurance programs that are below market rates as long as they cover all the costs (Laird 1999). Given that interest rates in the region are often quite high by international standards, providing export credit at unsubsidized rates that are lower than the ones prevailing in the domestic market is still highly beneficial for export firms, since the costs are closer to those faced by comparable companies elsewhere.

There are some Latin American governments that provide export firms with either direct export financing, for example, Colombia and Mexico, or with credit facilities for foreign clients, as is the case for Chile. Brazil has given high priority to providing export credit and guarantees (see Chapter 4 and Pedro da Motta Veiga, 1998). By contrast, there are other nations in the region that fail to provide export companies with financing facilities. Some other countries do have, presumably, an agency in charge of export financing. However, the resources allocated for this purpose are insignificant and go mainly to a few large firms. Therefore the impact of the export financing on export growth is negligible.

A lack of export financing is particularly harmful in those countries in which long-term loans are unavailable even for domestic transactions, due to market failures in the capital market. It is obvious that if companies have difficulties when applying for long-term loans for business in the country itself, they will face greater difficulties when trying to obtain financing for clients abroad.

Smaller and medium-sized firms often have limited access to financing because of their inability to provide adequate collateral. Providing smaller firms with loans that are not used directly by the companies, but which are deposited in the commercial bank providing the loan, can avoid this obstacle. Setting up this instrument decreases the barriers faced by smaller firms when they attempt to obtain export financing.

Governments should assign a high priority to establishing instruments that allow exporters access to financing. It is important to point out that this does not imply that financing should be provided at subsidized rates. Doing so would be incompatible with WTO rules, and would be a misallocation of government funds. What exporters need is access to export credit for working capital and for foreign clients at rates that are competitive internationally. Exporters' main problem with credit is that it is hard to get: this is particularly true for small and medium-sized firms. Large firms have a much wider range of financing options, at home and abroad.

Export credit can be supplied through various arrangements. One option is for the government to provide financing through a government export bank such as BANCOLDEX in Colombia or BANCOMEXT in Mexico. Another possibility is to channel resources through commercial banks that bid for export funds and to open lines of credit for purchasers abroad, as is done in Chile. Irrespective of what is the preferred arrangement, which may vary from one country to the next, the key issue that should not be obviated is the importance of allowing export companies access to export credit if increasing nontraditional exports has a high priority in the government's agenda.

At the same time, efforts should be carried out to set up instruments that allow companies to have access to insurance for nonpayment by importers. An export firm needs insurance against the risk of not being paid for its shipments by an importing company, that is, the insurance against commercial risk. This is one of the areas in which improving collaboration in the region would be very useful, since it could allow a substantial cut in the information costs needed for insuring against commercial risk.

Export companies also need to be protected from the political risk of an importing country's preventing payment being made, for example, when a nation decides to postpone paying all its commitments in foreign currencies. Insurance against this risk is still lacking in most countries. Some governments have considered establishing programs to cover this risk, but the progress is slow owing, partly, to the moral hazard risks resulting from insuring mainly exports to countries known to be in macroeconomic turmoil.

Specific Export Promotion Programs

If a government wishes to go further in promoting exports, it should contemplate carrying out the programs presented here. Nonetheless, it must be stressed that no single plan of action, even if it is very effective, is able to offset failure in applying the schemes discussed above. The instruments recommended here should be taken into account only after the issues mentioned above have been satisfactorily addressed.

A first proposal deals with seeking to simplify even further the formal regulations that apply to exporters. The first example is ALTEX, the scheme set up by the government of Mexico. This instrument allows companies with good reputations as exporters—regularly exporting a significant share of their output or large volumes of goods—to deal with highly streamlined export formalities.

Another option is to organize a program that provides small and medium-sized firms with assistance for carrying out the steps required for exporting, particularly when the firms have just started to sell abroad. This program is highly recommended for those countries that have to replace nonagricultural export subsidies by drawback and duty exemption to ensure compliance with the Uruguay Round Agreements. It is highly probable that smaller firms will face the greatest difficulties when they try to put together all the information needed to benefit from these instruments.

Together with all this, TPOs should follow up on a new kind of assistance, which is to help companies to be regularly in touch with their export markets. There are various ways of providing support in this matter. Colombian firms, for example, can rely on the offices that Proexport has in different countries, while Mexican companies benefit from assistance provided by BANCOMEXT's trade representatives. Another alternative is supplying financing and technical assistance, as ProChile is doing, so that groups of firms belonging to the same industry set up offices abroad. The ultimate goal is to encourage companies to have a permanent presence abroad, thus facilitating the transition from exporting intermittently to doing so continually. Having close links with the importing companies is particularly critical for firms exporting differentiated manufactured goods, since it enables them to keep up with the changes in demand.

At the same time, governments that have assigned a very high priority to increasing nontraditional exports can establish programs to further encourage exporting, under the terms of the *de minimis* clause of the Uruguay Round Agreements on subsidies and countervailing measures. This provision indicates that any countervailing duty investigation of a developing country (member of WTO) will be ended once it is determined that a subsidy level is not above 2% of unit value. The same will happen if the volume of the subsidized imports from a developing country is below a threshold of 4% of the imports of a product in the importing nation and, concurrently, the imports from all developing countries do not represent more than 9% of the imports (GATT 1994; Tussie 1997). Hence, it is still possible to encourage "pioneer" exports by firms exporting new products or to new markets.

Nonetheless, if the choice is made to establish such programs, it is critical that the following guidelines be taken into account:

- Programs should be aimed at firms that are exporting *new goods or to new markets*. This is the type of company that should be the main target of export promotion projects, with the goal of encouraging companies to significantly boost their export activity. This could be extended to providing funds for assisting firms in setting up offices abroad to enable them to export continually, since this can also be thought of as a shift in a firm's export activity.

- Financial assistance should be *moderate*. This is to attract companies that are truly willing to share the financial cost of the program—because of the high chances of success—while discouraging those firms that want only to be subsidized.
- Assistance provided by a program to specific companies should be *temporary*, with a termination date set at the beginning for a maximum period of two to three years. This is essential so that the assistance is genuinely a startup support and does not become a subsidy that has to be permanently maintained to ensure the continuation of export activity or even a firm's survival.
- Performance by a program should be periodically submitted to *external evaluations*. The program should be modified if there is a need to do so and terminated if it is yielding poor results. The assessment should determine whether the program encourages export growth and diversification and whether this trend will prevail after the program's assistance is completed.
- Projects should be *designed and managed jointly by public- and private-sector institutions,* such as exporter trade associations or private companies that have been awarded funds through an open bidding process. Export projects must have strong links with the private sector if they are to be successful.
- Programs must be *fully compatible with WTO rules*. If this condition is not met, an exporting country may have to face complaints channeled through the multilateral trade organization. Moreover, the country may be subject to retaliation—countervailing measures, for example—from its trading partners.

If it is not possible to make sure that programs aimed at triggering pioneer exports conform to these guidelines, it is better to not set them up and thereby avoid an inefficient allocation of government funds.

Policies for Upgrading Productivity of Domestic Firms

Governments should contemplate setting up or enhancing policies that foster productivity increases and upgrade export supply since such policies have, in the long run, the highest potential for contributing to an improvement in a country's ability to increase exports on a sustainable basis.

The importance of giving higher priority to productivity-upgrading programs is, to some extent, a consequence of the new WTO rules that entail eliminating nonagricultural export subsidies, while at the same time allowing some subsidies that are nonactionable. This includes subsidies that are not specific and those used for industrial research and precompetitive development, for assistance to disadvantaged regions, and for adaptation to new environmental regulations (GATT 1994).

One of the outcomes of the Uruguay Round Agreements is that policies that seek to promote widespread productivity increases will acquire a greater importance in the formulation of export promotion strategies (Agosín, Gitli, and Vargas 1996; Tussie and Lengyel 1998).

Export development programs recently set up by Chile and Colombia demonstrate the growing importance of productivity enhancement policies in government priorities. For instance, a chief guideline of the new export strategy designed by the government of Chile is to focus on adapting export products to the demand on international markets (Casanueva 1998). In Colombia, the Pastrana administration has taken steps in the same direction. This trend will most probably prevail in the coming years as more countries attempt to increase their export growth rates and adapt export promotion instruments to the Uruguay Round Agreements.

The new programs reflect the growing awareness of governments of the importance of increased productivity and adaptation of export supply to demand in international markets. They also show a compatibility with a new policy environment.[3]

With all this in mind, trade promotion organizations are broadening what they offer by including comprehensive trade development services designed to upgrade the productivity of domestic firms. The services include providing information on input sourcing and on assistance for adapting products, as well as support for improving product design and quality control (Bélisle 1998).

For instance, the government of Peru has stressed the importance of programs that allow firms to progressively adapt their products to the demand in international markets, instead of simply trying to export whatever goods are available. Prompex, the Peruvian TPO, has a program that provides assistance for quality certification and allows firms to benefit from services provided by international experts (Castillo 1998).

Programs that supply such services have positive results in the short run because they allow companies to boost their productivity. Moreover, the programs also have an extended positive effect in their signaling the need for given services and encouraging the provision of these services by private firms. All this provides an opportunity for a TPO to progressively allow the private sector to supply services and redirect its resources to newer programs needed by export firms. Such service provision schemes for export companies should be closely coordinated with any other programs a country may set up to upgrade productivity.

Another export boosting option is the promotion of companies that produce goods in high demand in export markets and of potentially profitable domestic manufacture. Fundación Chile, for example, set up firms to export salmon and berries in the 1980s. The companies, which successfully exported products that did not previously exist on the domestic market, were then sold to private entrepreneurs as a deliberate inducement to attract private investment.

Conclusions

Latin American and Caribbean countries, with the exception of Mexico, need to design new export promotion policies if they want to increase the growth rate of exports and move toward exporting goods with higher value added. The increasing challenges faced by export firms, the new policy environment, and the multilateral trade rules following the Uruguay Round Agreements demand that governments of the region design new export strategies that provide assistance for firms attempting to break into export markets.

This chapter has set forth recommendations with the potential of contributing to the design of the future export strategies. Nevertheless, the point should be made that whatever the export strategy ultimately chosen to assign high priority to increasing exports, there must be efforts to ensure that an export plan goes beyond a piecemeal collection of export promotion measures. An effective export promotion strategy that leads to export growth and diversification needs to be coherent and clearly signal that it fosters widespread increases in productivity. This implies that the other high-priority policies in a government's agenda are compatible with the goal of increasing exports and that the policies contribute to this goal.

Programs in an export promotion strategy should be assessed regularly to determine whether they are having an impact on individual firms. The questions that should be asked are whether managers know about these instruments and make use of them; whether the instruments are effective in assisting companies trying to start exporting; and whether the instruments encourage firms with experience in selling abroad to export continually. The use of the schemes by small and medium-sized companies should be an important yardstick for analyzing the schemes' adequacy. In addition, the proportion of exports that use these instruments should be determined. Information on the real cost of the instruments should be available—but this condition is in fact rarely met in most countries in the region. Information on the resources allocated to specific instruments is often difficult to obtain.

Any evaluation should go beyond the benefits for specific firms and establish whether these instruments/schemes are effective for increasing export growth, particularly that of nontraditional exports, and for encouraging a greater diversification of exports as well as exports of goods with greater value added. Effectiveness defined by these criteria should be the guideline for deciding whether an export promotion policy is successful. Latin American countries do have a tradition of setting up instruments that entrepreneurs come to believe should be permanent and that have no visible impact on export growth after the first few years.

The choices discussed here demonstrate that it is possible to design a strategy for encouraging companies to export new goods. A close collaboration between the public and private sectors regarding these issues would allow Latin American and Caribbean countries a higher rate of growth of exports with higher value added.

All in all, it is important that high-ranking civil servants working in TPOs be willing to go beyond their responsibilities of administrating export promotion programs and strive to ensure that a government has a coherent and comprehensive export strategy.

Last, it must be emphasized again that if a government wants to increase exports, the first tasks it must carry out are decreasing any antiexport bias and establishing a free-trade regime for export firms. Even the most effective export promotion program would be unable to compensate for the antiexport bias that results from high tariffs, nontariff barriers, significant export obstacles, rules that hinder competition in the domestic market, and an exchange rate that systematically appreciates far above the increases in productivity and the improvements in export performance.

Notes

1. See Larry Willmore (1996) for a discussion of the importance of allowing direct and indirect exporters access to the incentives granted to export processors.

2. For instance, only 0.6% of Mexico's exports in 1995 used the drawback. In the meantime, 29.3% of exports used the Programa de Importación Temporal para Producir Artículos de Exportación (PITEX), a duty exemption mechanism (Kate and Niels 1996).

3. See Wilson Peres (1997) and Joseph Ramos (1997) for a detailed presentation of policies seeking to increase productivity in Latin American countries.

References

Ablin, Eduardo, and Jorge M. Katz (1987), "From infant industry to technology exports: The Argentine experience in the international sale of industrial plants and re-engineering work," *Technology Generation in Latin American Manufacturing Industries*, Jorge Katz (ed.), Macmillan, London.

Agosín, Manuel (1997), *Trade and Growth in Chile: Past Performance and Future Prospects*, International Trade Unit, ECLAC, Santiago.

Agosín, Manuel (1993a), *Política Comercial en los Países Dinámicos de Asia: Aplicaciones a América Latina*, Division of Production, Productivity and Management, ECLAC, Santiago.

Agosín, Manuel (1993b), "Beneficios y Costos Potenciales para Chile de los Acuerdos de Libre Comercio," *Estudios Públicos* 52, Santiago.

Agosín, Manuel, and Ricardo Ffrench-Davis (1998), "La Inserción Externa de Chile: Experiencias Recientes y Desafíos," *Construyendo Opciones Propuestas Económicas y Sociales para el Cambio de Siglo*, René Cortazar and Joaquín Vial (eds.), Dolmen Ediciones, Santiago.

Agosín, Manuel, Eduardo Gitli, and Leiner Vargas (1996), *La promoción de exportaciones en Costa Rica: diagnóstico y recomendaciones para la próxima etapa*, Ministerio de Comercio Exterior de Costa Rica, San José.

Alcorta, Ludovico (1994), "The Impact of New Technologies on Scale in Manufacturing Industries: Issues and Evidence," *World Development* 22, 5, Oxford.

Alonso, Eduardo (1998), *Instrumentos y Políticas Exitosas en la Promoción del Comercio Exterior*, Conferencia Mundial de Organizaciones de Promoción del Comercio Exterior, Santiago.

Arrow, Kenneth J. (1962), "The economic implications of learning by doing," *Review of Economic Studies* XXIX (3), 80.

Bacha, E. (1995), "Plano Real: Uma avaliačao preliminar," *Revista do BNDES,* National Economic and Social Development Bank (BNDES), Rio de Janeiro.

Bacha, E. (1996), "Plano Real: Uma segunda Avaliačao," Río de Janeiro, Institute of Applied Economic Research, mimeo.

Banco Central de Chile (1999), *Informe Económico y Financiero,* Santiago.

Banco Central de Chile (1998), *Indicadores de Comercio Exterior,* Santiago.

BANCOMEXT (1996), *Annual Report*, Mexico City.

Barry, Nancy (1989), "Proceedings of the World Bank Annual Conference on Development Economics," *Supplement to the World Bank Economic Review and the World Bank Research Observer*, Washington, D.C.

Baumann, Renato (1994), *Exporting and the saga for competitiveness of Brazilian industry: 1992*, Working Paper No. 27, ECLAC, Santiago.

Bélisle, J. Denis (1998), *Trade Promotion Organizations: Past and Future, Keynote Address*, Second World Conference of Trade Promotion Organizations, Santiago.

Bhagwati, J., and T. N. Srinivasan (1983), *Lectures on International Trade*, MIT Press, Cambridge, Mass.

Bielschowsky, Ricardo (1994), *Two studies on transnational corporations in the Brazilian manufacturing sector: The 1980s and early 1990s*, Desarrollo Productivo series, 18, ECLAC, Santiago.

Bleany, Michael (1999), "Trade Reform, Macroeconomic Performance and Export Growth in Ten Latin American Countries 1979–95," *Journal of International Trade and Economic Development* 8, 1.

Bonelli, Regis (1997), "Exportações Não-Tradicionais no Brasil: Exito e Dificuldades," Division of Production, Productivity and Management, ECLAC, Santiago.

Brainard, S. Lael (1993), *A Simple Theory of Multinational Corporations and Trade with a Trade-off Between Proximity and Concentration,* NBER Working Paper 4269.

Brander, James A., and Barbara Spencer (1985), "Export subsidies and international market share rivalry," *Journal of International Economics* 18, North Holland.

Buitelaar, Rudolf M., Ramón Padilla, and Ruth Urrutia, (1999), "The in-bond assembly industry and technical change," *CEPAL Review* No. 67, Santiago.

Casanueva, Héctor (1998), *La Promoción de exportaciones en un mundo global*, Conferencia Mundial de Organizaciones de Promoción del Comercio Exterior, Santiago.

Castillo, Antonio (1998), *Instrumentos y Políticas Exitosas en la Promoción del Comercio de Bienes y Servicios*, Conferencia Mundial de Organizaciones de Promoción del Comercio Exterior, Santiago.

Castillo, Mario, Marco Dini, and Claudio Maggi (1994), *Reorganización industrial y estrategias competitivas en Chile*, Division of Production, Productivity and Management, ECLAC, Santiago.

Caves, R. E., and R. W. Jones (1985), *World Trade and Payments*, 4th ed., Little Brown.

Clements, Kenneth W., and Larry A. Sjaastad (1984), *How Protection Taxes Exporters*, Trade Policy Research Centre, London.

Clerides, Sofronis K., Saul Lach, and James R. Tybout (1998), "Is Learning by Exporting Important? Micro-dynamic Evidence from Colombia, Mexico and Morocco," *Quarterly Journal of Economics* CXIII, 3.

Consejo Superior de Comercio Exterior (1998), *Una Política de Desarrollo hacia afuera*, Bogotá.

Corbo, Vittorio, and José Miguel Sánchez (1984), *Impact on firms of the liberalization and stabilization policies in Chile: Some case studies*, Documento de trabajo No. 91, Pontificia Universidad Católica de Chile, Santiago.

DANE (Departamento Administrativo Nacional de Estadística) (1999a), Síntesis Estadística Semanal, January 18, Bogotá.

DANE (1999b), Síntesis Estadística Semanal, February 8, Bogotá.

DANE (1998a), Síntesis Estadística Semanal, August 23, Bogotá.

DANE (1998b), Síntesis Estadística Semanal, September 21, Bogotá.

DANE (1998c), Síntesis Estadística Semanal, September 28, Bogotá.

Devlin, Robert, and Ricardo Ffrench-Davis (1999), "Regional Integration in Latin America," *The World Economy* 22, 2, Oxford.

DIRECONBI (Dirección de Relaciones Económicas Bilaterales) (1994), "*Políticas comerciales de Chile*," Departamento de Estudios, Ministerio de Relaciones Exteriores de Chile, Santiago.

ECLAC (Economic Commission for Latin America and the Caribbean) (1999a), *Latin America and the Caribbean in the World Economy*, Santiago.

ECLAC (1999b), *Statistical Yearbook for Latin America and the Caribbean, 1998 Edition*, Santiago.

ECLAC (1999c), *Economic Survey of Latin America and the Caribbean 1998–1999*, Santiago.

ECLAC (1999d), *Chile 1998*, Santiago.

ECLAC (1998a), *Module for Analyzing Growth in International Commerce* (MAGIC), Santiago.

ECLAC (1998b), *Statistical Yearbook for Latin America and the Caribbean, 1997 Edition*, Santiago.

Esser, Klaus, et al., (1995), *Nuevas Tendencias del fomento a la exportación. Exigencias al concepto y a los instrumentos. El ejemplo del Uruguay*, Estudios e Informes 11, Instituto Alemán del Desarrollo, Berlin.

Ethier, Wilfred (1979), "Internationally Decreasing Costs and World Trade," *Journal of International Economics* 9, North-Holland Publishing Company.

Ffrench-Davis, Ricardo (1989), "El conflicto entre la deuda y el crecimiento en Chile: Tendencias y perspectivas," *Colección Estudios* CIEPLAN 6, Santiago.

Ffrench-Davis, Ricardo (1980), "Liberalización de las importaciones: La experiencia chilena en 1973–1979," *Colección Estudios* CIEPLAN 4, Santiago.

Ffrench-Davis, Ricardo, P. Leiva, and R. Madrid (1992), "Liberalización comercial y crecimiento. La experiencia de Chile, 1973–89," *Pensamiento Iberoamericano* 21, Madrid.

Fortuna, E. (1994), *Mercado financiero: productos y servicios,* 4th ed., Quality Mark Editora, Rio de Janeiro.

Garay, Luis Jorge et al., (1998), *Colombia: Estructura industrial e internacionalización 1967–1996*, Departamento Nacional de Planeación, Colciencias, Consejería Económica y de Competitividad, Ministerio de Comercio Exterior, Ministerio de Hacienda y Crédito Público, Proexport Colombia, Bogotá.

García, Pablo, Patricio Meller, and Andrea Repetto (1996), "Las Exportaciones como Motor de Crecimiento: La Evidencia Chilena," *El Modelo Exportador Chileno: Crecimiento y Equidad*, Patricio Meller (ed.), CIEPLAN, Santiago.

GATT (General Agreement on Tariffs and Trade) (1994), *Final Act Embodying the Results of the Uruguay Round of Multilateral Trade Negotiations,* Marrakesh.

GATT (1991), *Examen de las políticas comerciales*, Geneva.

Helleiner, G. K. (1995), *Manufacturing for Export in the Developing World, Problems and Possibilities*, United Nations University, Routledge, London.

Helpman, Elhanan (1989), "The noncompetitive theory of international trade and trade policy," *Proceedings of the World Bank Annual Conference on Development Economics*, Washington, D.C.

Hobday, Michael (1995), *Innovation in East Asia: The challenge to Japan*, Edward Elgar Publishing Limited, Hants, England.

Horstmann, Ignatius J., and James R. Markusen (1992), "Endogenous Market Structures in International Trade," *Journal of International Economics* 32, North Holland.

Iglesias, R. (1996), "A evolução recente das exportacões brasileiras," mimeo.

Kate, Adriaan ten (1998), "Response of Manufacturing Exports to Import Liberalization in Mexico: Is There a Second Wave," *The Handbook of*

Latin American Trade in Manufactures, Montague J. Lord (ed.), Edward Elgar, United Kingdom/United States.

Kate, Adriaan ten, and Gunnar Niels (1996), *El Entorno de Política Económica del Desempeño Exportador de México*, Division of Production, Productivity and Management, ECLAC, Santiago.

Katz, Jorge, and Gustavo Burachik (1997), La industria farmacéutica y farmoquímica argentina en los años noventa, *Apertura económica y desregulación en el mercado de medicamentos*, Jorge Katz (comp.), ECLAC/CIID (Centro Internacional de Investigaciones para el Desarrollo)/Alianza Editorial, Buenos Aires.

Katz, Jorge M. (1987), "Domestic technology generation in LDCs: a review of research findings," *Technology Generation in Latin American Manufacturing Industries*, Jorge M. Katz (ed.), Macmillan, London.

Keesing, Donald B., and Sanjaya Lall (1992), "Marketing manufactured exports from developing countries: Learning sequences and public support," *Trade Policy, Industrialization and Development*, Gerald K. Helleiner (ed.), World Institute for Development Economics Research (WIDER) of the United Nations University, Clarendon, Oxford.

Krueger, Anne O. (1985), "The Experience and Lessons of Asia's Super Exporters," *Export-Oriented Development Strategies, The Success of Five Newly Industrializing Countries*, Vittorio Corbo, Anne O. Krueger, and Fernando Ossa (eds.), Westview, Boulder, Colo., London.

Krugman, Paul (1993), "Free trade: A loss of (theoretical) nerve? The narrow and broad arguments for free trade," *American Economic Review*, Anaheim, Calif.

Krugman, Paul (1987), "The Narrow Moving Band, the Dutch Disease and the Competitive Consequences of Mrs. Thatcher," *Journal of Development Economics* 27, Elsevier Science Publishers, North Holland.

Krugman, Paul, and Maurice Obstfeld (1994), *International Economics, Theory and Policy*, 3d Edition, HarperCollins College Publishers, New York.

Laird, Sam (1999), "Export Policy and the WTO," *Journal of International Trade and Economic Development* 8, 1.

Lucas, Robert E. (1993), " Making a Miracle," *Econometrica* 61, 2.

Macario, Carla (1998a), *Learning and Exporting: Evidence from Successful Export Firms in Mexico*, Division of Production, Productivity and Management, ECLAC, Santiago.

Macario, Carla (1998b), *Chile: Learning and Economies of Scale in Export Firms Compared to Non-Export Firms*, Division of Production, Productivity and Management, ECLAC, Santiago.

Macario, Carla (1998c), "Chile: From policies that subsidize exports to policies that enhance competitiveness," *Integration and Trade*, Institute for the Integration of Latin America and the Caribbean, Inter-American Development Bank 2, 4/5, Buenos Aires.

Macario, Carla (1998d), *Why and How Do Firms Export: Evidence from Successful Export Firms in Colombia*, Division of Production, Productivity and Management, ECLAC, Santiago.

Macario, Carla (1995), "América Latina: competitividad y políticas de promoción de exportaciones," *Comercio Exterior* 45, 3, Mexico City.

Máttar, Jorge (1998), "Export Promotion in Mexico," *Integration and Trade* 4/5, Institute for the Integration of Latin America and the Caribbean, Inter-American Development Bank, Buenos Aires.

Máttar, Jorge (1996), Desempeño exportador y competitividad internacional: Algunos ejercicios CAN para México, *Comercio Exterior* 6, 3, Mexico City.

Máttar, Jorge, and Wilson Peres (1997), "La Política Industrial y de Comercio Exterior en México," *Políticas de Competitividad Industrial, América Latina y el Caribe en los años noventa*, Wilson Peres (ed.), Siglo XXI Editores, Mexico City.

Monge, Ricardo (1998), "Costa Rica's Experience in the Area of Export Promotion," *Integration & Trade* 4/5, Inter-American Development Bank, Buenos Aires.

Motta Veiga, Pedro da (1998), "Export Promotion Policies in Brazil: Background, Current Situation and Main Trends," *Integration & Trade* 4/5, Inter-American Development Bank, Buenos Aires.

Neary, J. Peter (1994), "Cost asymmetries in international subsidy games: Should governments help winners or losers?" *Journal of International Economics* 37, 3–4, Elsevier, Netherlands.

Ocampo, José Antonio (1994), "Trade Policy and Industrialization in Colombia, 1967–91," *Trade Policy and Industrialization in Turbulent Times*, G. K. Helleiner (ed.), UNU/WIDER, Routledge, London.

Ocampo, José Antonio (1993), "New theories of international trade and trade policy in developing countries," *Trade and Growth, New Dilemmas in Trade Policy*, Manuel Agosín and Diane Tussie (eds.), St. Martin's Press, New York.

Ocampo, José Antonio, and Leonardo Villar (1995), "Colombian Manufactured Exports, 1967–91," *Manufacturing for Exporting in the Developing World, Problems and Possibilities*, G. K. Helleiner (ed.), Routledge, London.

Ochoa, Pablo (1998), "Políticas e Instrumentos de Promoción de Exportaciones en Colombia," *Integración y Comercio* 4/5, Instituto para la Integración de América Latina y el Caribe (INTAL), Inter-American Development Bank, Buenos Aires.

OMC (Organización Mundial del Comercio)(1997a), *Examen de las políticas comerciales, Chile*, Informe de la Secretaría, Geneva.

OMC (1997b), *Examen de las políticas comerciales, Colombia 1996*, Informe de la Secretaría, Geneva.

Pardo, Magdalena (1996), *Diseño de Políticas para el Fortalecimiento de la Capacidad de Innovación Tecnológica y Elevación de la Competitividad Internacional en el Ámbito Empresarial Latinoamericano: El Caso Colombiano*, Division of Production, Productivity and Management, ECLAC, Santiago.

Peres, Wilson (1997) (ed.), *Las Políticas de Competitividad Industrial en América Latina y el Caribe en los Años Noventa*, Siglo XXI, Mexico City.

Pinheiro, A. C. (1996), "The Brazilian Economy in the Nineties: Retrospect and Policy Challenges," National Economic and Social Development Bank, mimeo.

ProChile (1997), *Análisis de las Exportaciones Chilenas: Primer Semestre 1997*, Santiago.

Ramos, Joseph (1997), "La Política de Desarrollo Productivo en Economías Abiertas," *Las Políticas de Competitividad Industrial en América Latina y el Caribe en los Años Noventa*, Wilson Peres (ed.), Siglo XXI, Mexico City.

Ramos, Joseph (1986), *Neoconservative Economics in the Southern Cone of Latin America, 1973–1983*, Johns Hopkins University Press, Baltimore.

Rhee, Yung Whee (1985), *Instruments for Export Policy and Administration, Lessons from the East Asian Experience*, World Bank Staff Working Papers No. 725, World Bank, Washington, D.C.

Roberts, M. J., and James R. Tybout (1997), *What Makes Exports Boom?* World Bank, Washington, D.C.

Rodrik, Dani (1992), "Closing the productivity gap: Does trade liberalization really help?" *Trade Policy, Industrialization and Development: New Perspectives*, Gerald K. Helleiner (ed.), World Institute for Development Economics Research (WIDER) of the United Nations University, Clarendon Press, Oxford.

Rodrik, Dani (1988), "Imperfect competition, scale economies and trade policy in developing countries," *Trade Policy Issues and Empirical Analysis*, Robert E. Baldwin (ed.), University of Chicago Press, Chicago.

Ros, Jaime (1994), "Mexico's Trade and Industrialization Since 1960," *Trade Policy and Industrialization in Turbulent Times*, G. K. Helleiner (ed.), Routledge, London.

Rosales, Osvaldo (1999), "El impacto de la crisis asiática en la economía

chilena," *America Latina*, Centro Europeo di Studi sulla Democratizzazione, Università di Bologna.
Servicio Nacional de Aduanas (1994), *Boletín Oficial*, Santiago.
Tussie, Diana (1997), *Trade Policies and Commitments in the World Trade Organization*, International Trade Unit, ECLAC, Santiago.
Tussie, Diana, and Miguel Lengyel (1998), "WTO Commitments on Export Promotion," *Integration & Trade* 4/5, Inter-American Development Bank, Buenos Aires.
Westphal, Larry E. (1998), "The Pendulum Swings—An Apt Analogy?" *World Development* 26, 12, Washington, D.C.
Willmore, Larry (1996), *Export Processing in the Caribbean: Lessons from Four Case Studies*, Working Paper No. 42, ECLAC, Santiago.
World Bank (1999), *Global Commodity Markets* 7, 1, Washington, D.C.
WTO (World Trade Organization) (1999), Press Release April 16, 1999.
WTO (1998a), *International Trade Statistics, Annual Report 1998*, Geneva.
WTO (1998b), *Annual Report 1998*, Special Topic: Globalization and Trade, Geneva.
Young, Alwyn (1991), "Learning by doing and the dynamic effects of international trade," *Quarterly Journal of Economics* CVI, 2, MIT Press, Cambridge, Mass.

Index

About the Book

Although Latin American and Caribbean countries have assigned a high priority to increasing exports in recent years—substantially transforming their economies in the process—export performance in most cases remains deficient. This book investigates why this is so, identifying the policies that determine successes and failures in Brazil, Chile, Colombia, and Mexico.

Each country case study focuses systematically on the macroeconomic environment, its trade and export promotion policies, and the influence of those policies on firms' export behavior. The authors also consider the learning experiences of firms that successfully change their practices in order to compete in global markets. A concluding chapter offers policy recommendations for enhancing export performance within the bounds of the Uruguay Round Agreements.

Carla Macario is economic affairs officer with the UN Economic Commission for Latin America and the Caribbean (ECLAC) in Chile. **Regis Bonelli** is a research associate at IPEA—Instituto de Pesquisa Econômica Aplicada (Institute for Applied Economic Research)—an agency of the Brazilian Ministry of Planning and Budget. **Adriaan ten Kate** is director for economic studies at the Competition Commission of Mexico. **Gunnar Niels** is a consultant with Oxford Economic Research Associates.